IN FOCUS

BELIZE

A Guide to the People, Politics and Culture

Ian Peedle

LATIN AMERICA BUREAU

INTERLINK BOOKS
NEW YORK

The edition first published in 2004

In the U.S.:

Interlink Books
An imprint of Interlink Publishing Group, Inc.
46 Crosby Street, Northampton, Massachusetts, 01060
www.interlinkbooks.com

Library of Congress Cataloging-in-Publication Data

Peedle, Ian,
    Belize in focus: a guide to the people, politics and culture /
    by Ian Peedle
    p. cm.
    Includes bibliographical references.
    ISBN: 1-56656-284-8   (pbk)
    1. Belize - Guidebooks. 2. Belize - Description and travel.
    I. Title
    F1443.5.P44   1999
    917.28204'5 - dc21   99-18563
                                                               CIP

In the U.K.:

Latin America Bureau (Research and Action) Ltd,
1 Amwell Street, London EC1R 1UL

The Latin America Bureau is an independent research and publishing
organization. It works to broaden public understanding of issues of
human rights and social and economic justice in Latin America and the
Caribbean.

A CIP catalogue record for this book is available from the British
Library
ISBN: 1 899365 35 4

Editing: James Ferguson
Cover photograph: Barry Lewis/Network
Cover design: Andy Dark
Design: Liz Morrell
Cartography and diagrams: Catherine Pyke

Already published in the *In Focus* series:
Argentina, Bolivia, Brazil, Chile, Colombia, Costa Rica, Cuba,
Dominican Republic, Eastern Caribbean, Ecuador, Guatemala, Jamaica,
Mexico, Peru, Venezuela

Printed and bound in Korea

CONTENTS

INTRODUCTION: DIVERSITY AND UNCERTAINTY

Belize is a fascinating and diverse country. An increasing number of tourist guidebooks concentrate on the wonders of its environment and its pristine natural resources that make it an attractive destination for North American and European tourists. Yet, as well as its unmatched natural beauty, Belize also contains urban squalor and rural poverty to match anywhere else in the world. This is a country of contrasts, which behind the mask of the tourist images, reveals a more complex character than the welcoming, friendly and straightforward face usually presented to the outside world.

The guidebooks do, of course, have a point. Belize's natural resources are among the most impressive on the planet. The brilliantly colorful underwater world centered on the longest barrier reef in the Western Hemisphere is quite magical. And the magnificence of Belize's lush green eternal forest landscape is equally breathtaking.

Belize is a country where the modern and ancient sit side by side – where it is possible to use the internet in an air-conditioned office one minute and sit on the dirt floor of a Mayan thatched hut practically the next. An air of calm and openness has made it a haven for refugees and migrants from all over the world. Successive waves of immigration have created a unique multi-cultural society at the crossroads of the English-speaking Caribbean and Central America.

Belize's society has evolved slowly and largely peacefully and with a tolerance that can seem quite remarkable to the outsider. A diverse population is the consequence of long unbroken Maya settlement of the land, European imperialism, the influx of refugees from Central American and Mexican civil wars, Garifuna and Mennonite settlement, and an ongoing Economic Citizenship Program. Despite the resulting diversity, Belize's ethnic communities enjoy a mostly peaceful and productive partnership, even if indigenous groups voice well-founded grievances about land and identity.

The natural beauty and relaxed atmosphere make Belize a special place to live and visit. With only just over 220,000 people inhabiting 8,800 square miles it remains relatively unspoiled despite the growing pains it is experiencing as a newly independent country – increases in population, and the growth of tourism and plantation agriculture are putting more pressure on Belize's natural resources.

Belize is now entering one of the most challenging periods in its history. Guatemala's territorial claim on the country remains unresolved, even though Guatemala has recognized Belizean independence. The paving of the Southern Highway, the country's last major dirt highway, will bring

A view through the mangroves   *James Beveridge*

unprecedented change to the south of the country. The possibility, under current free-trade doctrine, of the removal of subsidies for Belize's traditional exports will have an enormous impact on the national economy. Belize is, without doubt, a country in transition.

This guide explores the makeup of modern Belize – its people, environment, culture, economy, and history and assesses how this largely rural economy is struggling to prepare for a future that is becoming ever more uncertain.

1   INFLUENCES AND ENVIRONMENT: THE FORMING OF MODERN BELIZE

Belize has always struggled to find its own national identity. Surrounded as it is by strongly defined and developed cultures, modern Belize has been shaped as much by external forces as by its own internal dynamics. While nationalist politicians, especially the father of modern Belize, George Price, seized on a romantic Mayan cultural ideal in an attempt to unite different population groups around one single cultural theme, the reality was far different. Since the arrival of Europeans in the sixteenth century the Maya have been a disadvantaged and declining part of Belize's population, and the country's identity is marked more than anything by its ability to absorb other people and cultures into a loose-knit national community.

Early History

Belize was part of the great Mayan civilization that spread throughout the Central American region. When the first Europeans arrived in the early sixteenth century they encountered a Mayan society that had undergone a dramatic transformation since its heyday some six hundred years earlier. Contact with the Europeans was to have a devastating effect on the remaining Maya through disease, slavery and fighting. Many died and many fled, seeking refuge in more remote areas, especially in Guatemala.

Spain and Britain set out the boundaries for modern Belize in the 1700s in the form of logging concessions given to British settlers by Spain, which claimed sovereignty but did not settle the land. These settlers were mainly ex-pirates who were gradually being forced out of their old trade as European governments abandoned their support for their own national privateers and sought to stamp out piracy.

British involvement in Belize grew as the settlers called for protection from attacks by the Spanish and the remaining Mayan population. British armed forces were sent on a number of occasions, including the most famous of Belize's battles, the Battle of St. George's Caye in 1798, which marked the end of Spanish claims to the territory.

Belize's People

In 1871, some two centuries after the settlers first landed and fifty years after Belize's Mexican and Central American neighbors had achieved independence from Spain, Belize was officially declared a British Crown Colony.

By this time the population had grown significantly and the colony's economy had developed almost exclusively around forest products, mainly mahogany, chicle and logwood. A large number of Africans were brought as slaves by the settlers from other British territories in the Caribbean, and as part of an agreement with Spain, more than 2,000 people had relocated to Belize in 1787 from the English-speaking settlement of Mosquito Shore on the Nicaraguan/Honduran coast.

At the turn of the nineteenth century, Garifuna – the so-called "Black Caribs" deported in 1797 by the British from St. Vincent to Roatán off the Central American coast – began settling along Belize's southern coastline, and in the mid-nineteenth century, there was an influx into northern Belize of thousands of *mestizo* (of mixed Spanish and Maya descent) and Maya refugees fleeing the Caste War in Mexico's Yucatán peninsular. This war (in Spanish known as the *Guerra de Castes*) began in 1847 during the Mexican War between Mexico and the U.S., and was fought between the Maya of the Yucatán against non-natives who threatened the traditional Mayan way of life. Many Maya and mestizos fled south as a result of the war and settled in Belize and in the southern Yucatecan state of Quintana Roo.

Following the abolition of slavery in the nineteenth century, a small number of Indian and Chinese indentured laborers arrived in Belize, and in the early twentieth century Palestinian, Lebanese and Syrian Arabs also began arriving, fleeing political unrest in the Middle East.

Further significant population expansion occurred in the mid-twentieth century with the arrival of Mennonites from Mexico. These skilled farmers quickly established "colonies"– small self-contained farming communities – in the west and north of the country.

Political Development

As the population expanded, and with the increased political involvement of non-whites, political power passed from the handful of original settlers and their descendants – the "forestocracy" – to the British colonial administrations of the nineteenth and early twentieth centuries. These administrations were dominated by the colonial and business elite, particularly the Belize Estate and Produce Company (BEC), which had grown to be the major force in the colony. These colonial governments also gave a growing class of professional educated Creoles – Belize's colored and black elite – their first taste of political power.

The rise of nationalist politics in the 1930s mirrored developments elsewhere in the Caribbean and was given further impetus by a terrible hurricane that hit Belize in 1931 and a fire that swept through the capital city in the same year. A currency devaluation that halved the value of the country's economy was the event that led to the creation of Belize's first political parties, including the party that was to dominate political life in Belize until the 1980s, the People's United Party (PUP).

Formed in 1950, the PUP was led by George Price, and emerged to spearhead, the campaign for Belizean independence. Self-government for Belize was achieved in 1964, at the same time most of the other British Caribbean Crown Colonies were gaining their full independence. It was the unresolved problem of Guatemala's territorial claim on Belize, and the issue of its security that delayed full independence until 1981. Since Guatemala appeared to be serious about taking over Belize as soon as the British left, and since Belize itself had no armed forces, it needed outside protection. So after independence, the British agreed to maintain a full-time army base in Belize, which remained until 1994. Some suspect that both countries knew that Guatemala never really intended to attack, and that this continued British military presence was actually part of a wider regional strategy worked out with the U.S.

Central American Crises

The late 1970s and early 1980s saw modern Belize's greatest demographic change when as many as 40,000 Central Americans crossed into the country in search of refuge from civil war, oppression and economic hardship. Belize's recent history has been one of coming to terms with this population explosion – new Central American immigrants account for about 25 percent of the total population – and its economic, political and social consequences.

The impact of absorbing so many so quickly was partially offset by increases in foreign aid being made available to Belize in the 1980s. The international organization which provided most assistance to Belize during the crisis years was the United Nations High Commission for Refugees (UNHCR). Belize was also central to the regional political strategy of the U.S. during this time – it was used as a base of sorts, establishing a major diplomatic presence, joint military operations, and propaganda machinery such as a Voice of America transmitter – and American presence and funding in Belize reflected this importance. As the Central American crises were resolved in the 1990s, organizations such as UNHCR began cutting back and by 1998 had almost ceased operations. U.S. involvement in Belize also rapidly declined during the second half of the 1990s.

Emerging Economy

During the second half of the twentieth century, the export-oriented economy was successfully diversified from its forest base into sugar, citrus and banana production, as well as tourism. Although the economy still remains very vulnerable to external forces, Belize's small population mitigates against the growth of a more diversified local economy.

Despite the high profits that were earned during the colonial era, investments in infra-structure were neglected, and Belize has had to rely heavily on

British soldiers visit Maya ruins   *James Beveridge*

foreign aid to put in the roads, electricity, and other infrastructure necessary for a modern economy.

Attempting to end this reliance on foreign assistance, the government has sought ways to diversify the economy further and to generate its own revenues. The most controversial scheme is the Economic Citizenship Program (ECP), begun in the late 1980s. This program has been mainly aimed at Taiwanese nationals, who pay up to $40,000 each for Belizean nationality. The ECP has led to the latest bout of population growth, with new purpose-built communities inhabited by Taiwanese-Belizeans springing up alongside major highways. The new immigrants have also purchased large tracts of land. This is the first time since the original settlers that a group of new immigrants have wielded such economic and political power and despite the obvious economic benefits, many Belizeans are unhappy and question the wisdom of the passports-for-sale policy.

Shifting Alliances

The impact of European, especially British, involvement in Belize was tremendous and the national institutions and colonial culture put in place during this period are still very visible today. The inheritance includes a close relationship with the countries of the English-speaking Caribbean, especially Jamaica. But new regional alliances driven by changing political conditions and the free-trade paradigm are overtaking post-colonial allegiances. Belize has signed up to be part of an Americas-wide free trade area to be established early in the new millennium. It is also forging closer political, economic and cultural links with its immediate neighbors, most notably Mexico, and is being drawn ever closer into regional Central American political and economic activity as relations with Guatemala improve.

Belize's Westminster-style political systems and structures were introduced by the British colonial government with very little consideration for political realities within Belize's unique society. A growing number of opponents believe the system in operation has been divisive and inefficient and has led to widespread abuse of power. Reformers are calling for a presidential-style system of government, more independent checks and balances over the activities of government ministers, and more effective decentralization of decision-making.

The legal system in Belize also remains closely associated with the British model, and the Judicial Committee of the British Privy Council is Belize's highest Court of Appeal. The most famous recent case involving the Privy Council culminated early one morning in 1995.

Hard-liners in the Belize government were determined to show they were serious in the fight against violent crime by carrying out the death penalty on two men sentenced for murder. The two men were driven from their cells to the gallows early on the morning of the planned execution. As final preparations were made, the men's lawyer waited anxiously for the outcome of an appeal to the Privy Council in London. The London judges, with literally only minutes to spare, finally faxed through a stay of execution, which was rushed by the lawyer to the Belize authorities, who spared the men's lives.

This episode gave rise to heated debate on the need for reform of this system; many asked why judges in London should be called upon to decide the fate of Belize's criminals when they knew nothing of the circumstances in Belize. Most Belizeans favor retention of some form of independent final court of appeal but would prefer a regional Caribbean judicial body.

External Influences

There are still significant traces of the colonial era in Belizean life. These include the attitudes and experiences of older Belizeans who were brought up under colonial rule, an education system that has its roots in the British system, and the annual scholarships awarded to Belizeans to study in the UK. British sports such as cricket are still popular, especially in rural Creole communities, and many Belizeans have family connections to the UK either through migration or through inter-marriage, especially with British soldiers stationed in Belize.

But while the British influence has had a great impact, the dominant external influence on modern Belize undoubtedly comes from the U.S. The early twentieth century saw the U.S. begin to replace the European powers as the principal political and economic force in the region.

An old British pillar box in Belize City   *James Beveridge*

The U.S. position with respect to Belize was complicated by its policy in Guatemala. In the 1950s, Belize's most influential nationalist politicians saw the U.S. as their natural economic and political ally, singing "God Bless America" and displaying the stars and stripes at their rallies and demonstrations. But the U.S. itself was more anxious to protect its valuable relationship with Guatemala, and did not press for Belize's territorial independence.

American economic involvement in Belize was also slower than hoped for by the PUP, which in the 1960s expected U.S. investment to end British economic dominance. Until fairly recently most American investment went into the purchasing of land for speculative purposes, but a growing number of U.S. businessmen now invest and work hands-on in more productive activities, particularly in tourism, agriculture and garment manufacturing.

Up until the mid-1990s, the major source of U.S. government funding for Belize was probably its aid program, channeled through the U.S. Agency for International Development (USAID). Funding peaked at $20 million annually during the late 1980s when the troubles in Central America were at their height, but the end of the crises led to the closing of USAID's operations in Belize in 1996.

The Drugs Boomerang

British and U.S. anti-drug efforts in the Caribbean in the 1960s and 1970s concentrated on forcing farmers out of marijuana production. Belize had been a major marijuana producer and the presence of British troops in the country assisted the anti-narcotics campaign. The continuous spraying of suspected marijuana-growing areas had the desired effect of driving farmers out of marijuana production. In the process, they also ruined attempts that some farmers had made to diversify into honey production. With marijuana and honey production no longer options, the door opened invitingly for the more lucrative and more dangerous business of cocaine smuggling. Belize, ideally placed between Colombia, Mexico and the U.S., quickly grew into one of the main transit routes for cocaine from Latin to North America.

Reports are rife of light planes landing in the dead of night on major highways to make drug-related transactions. In fact, the problem became so bad on the Northern Highway that the government had to erect pillars along the roadside to prevent planes landing. And there are plentiful accounts of poor and struggling fishermen turned rich and boastful owners of expensive speedboats after "happening upon" bales of cocaine washed up alongside their lobster traps. But the downside of the drug money, which undoubtedly finds its way into Belize's economy, is the misery caused by drug addiction – crack cocaine addiction is a major problem in Belize City and is behind much of the violent crime that has plagued the city for the past decade.

Again, outsiders seem to be holding the strings; in the 1990s there were a number of spectacular inland and offshore drug busts in Belize, usually involving Colombian and Mexican nationals. The drug smugglers, however, seem able to routinely escape custody, amid press reports about the complicity of Belizean government officials – from law enforcement agents up to the ministerial level.

Stolen Cars and Gang Culture

The other smuggling activity against which the U.S. has sought Belize's assistance is the importing into Belize of stolen American vehicles. Belizeans regularly travel to the U.S. to purchase vehicles, which are then driven down to Belize through Mexico. In fact, this is probably the route by which most of Belize's vehicles enter the country.

In the late 1990s, the U.S. requested that Belize be more vigilant in identifying stolen vehicles crossing its borders. This request led to some fierce exchanges between U.S. diplomats and Belize government ministers, especially the Foreign Minister, Dean Barrow. Barrow pointed out that the cars were stolen in the U.S. and had already crossed the U.S. and Mexican borders before reaching Belize. He asked how, if these two countries with all the resources at their disposal were unable to prevent the crime, Belize, with its limited resources, could be expected to do any better.

The political altercations over the smuggling of drugs and stolen vehicles have exposed the sometimes uneasy relationship that exists between the two countries. The U.S., faced with what it saw as Belize's lackluster response in dealing with these problems, threatened withdrawal of a range of economic assistance. Aware of the profoundly negative implications of

Crashed light airplane in the rainforest

James Beveridge

this breakdown in relations, the Belize government began to make the right noises and fell into step with U.S. wishes.

While the U.S. is worried about Belize's response to smuggling of vehicles and drugs, Belize has become increasingly concerned with a growth in violent crime imported from the U.S. The late 1980s and 1990s saw an explosion in gang-related street crime in Belize, much of which was linked to the drug trade. Fuelled by the deportation from the U.S. of Belizeans who had been convicted of criminal activities, violent street crime escalated out of control in the early 1990s, as Belize City's poor black youth tried to swagger and shoot their way to a better future.

Belize City was hardest hit and substantial resources were needed to bring the problem under control. The availability, since the late 1980s, of pirated American cable television gave young Belizeans regular access to a glamorized violent street culture, dominated by young American blacks and Hispanics. Many Belizeans also have family members in the States and through them receive U.S. culture firsthand (most of the estimated 50,000 expatriate Belizeans live in the three major cities of Los Angeles, New York and Chicago).

Violent street crimes do appear to have decreased in the late 1990s, partly due to government initiatives that have provided some alternative opportunities for young people. Other factors likely to have caused a drop

14

in gangland activities are the death and/or arrest of many of the leading gang members, and the small size of Belize City, which does not offer the same inner-city protection as Kingston or Los Angeles.

Geography
Northern Belize: Sugar and Nature

The northern Region is undoubtedly the best developed area of Belize, enjoying good infrastructure and services. Although the poor quality of soils in these low-lying flatlands limits the development of agricultural activity, this is where Belize's most important agricultural crop, sugar, is grown. As well as significant for their sugar output, the northern plains are increasingly recognized as an important wetland and forest habitat and are home to a number of wildlife reserves, including the famous Crooked Tree reserve, and Belize's largest private forest reserve, the 228,000-acre Rio Bravo Conservation and Management Area.

Corozal Town, close by the border with Mexico, is an attractive small coastal community, with a developing tourism industry, though the local economy is primarily based on the sugar industry. The Belize government is also attempting, so far with limited success, to establish a Free Trade Zone just north of Corozal Town to take advantage of the North American Free Trade Agreement (NAFTA), which encompasses Mexico. Now, with the recent Summit of the Americas decision to create an Americas-wide free trade zone, this initiative may well prove unnecessary.

Orange Walk Town is Belize's second commercial center after Belize City, and again its economic life is based on the sugar industry, although it is also widely rumored to be the capital of Belize's drug trade. Outside of these two main towns, the rest of the population live in small villages, most of which are scattered along the Northern Highway. Belize's commercial center, Belize City, is home to about one-third of the population and continues to dominate Belize politically and economically.

Changing Faces

The two northernmost districts, Corozal and Orange Walk, are predominantly mestizo – of mixed Spanish and Mayan descent – a result of the Guerra de Castes immigration in the 1840s. The Belize District, on the other hand, is the stronghold of Belize's black Creole population, although more and more mestizos are moving into the Belize District in search of work and the city life that Belize City has to offer.

Unlike in most other countries, the rural population has been growing at a faster rate than the population in the urban centers, as a result of emigration of mainly Creole Belizeans to the U.S. and immigration into rural areas from Belize's Central American neighbors.

Swing Bridge in Belize City

James Beveridge

As the rural Hispanic population continues to grow, Belize's rural Creole population based along the Belize River Valley faces hard times. These communities, which nearly all grew out of old logging camps, face a slow death as young people leave in droves searching for job opportunities in Belize City or in the U.S. Although the Belize government is trying to stem the problem, its special initiatives aimed at developing agricultural production and promoting Creole culture are having only a limited effect.

Belize City—Swamp Thing

Belize City, which was allegedly raised by pirates from the swamp on top of empty rum bottles, has a reputation for being one of the Caribbean's more dangerous and dirty destinations. Until recently, overflowing open drains ran along the sides of crowded narrow streets and escalating violent crime meant the city's reputation was well justified. Violence is on the decrease, however, and Belize City has recently been under the planner's scalpel for a much needed facelift. The drains have been covered and the newly paved streets even boast sidewalks.

Even so, much of the downtown area remains a congested snarl of narrow one-way streets. Pedestrians, cyclists, and vehicles melt seamlessly into one moving mass. Most vehicles are either tyrannical American gas-guzzling taxis or overbearing four-wheel drive utilities and pick-ups that are more at home on rural dirt roads than in the city center. Cyclists and pedestrians weave in and out of the constant traffic flow in a raucous dance with death which is not for the faint-hearted.

Still, the city has moments of welcome tranquillity. The crowd of fishing boats by the Swing Bridge (the world's oldest manually operated swing bridge, which is duly cranked open twice a day to let tall craft along the Belize River) makes for a colorful crossroads between the city and the offshore calm of the Caribbean sea. The adjacent Maritime Museum gives visitors the chance to learn something of the history of this marriage with the sea.

And Belize has plenty of examples of traditional Caribbean wooden architecture despite losses from hurricanes and fires. The Paslow building, again by the Swing Bridge, and the Governor's House, which is open to the public, are probably the best the city has to offer.

Because of the threat of hurricanes, modern buildings are nearly all built from concrete. Building costs are high because of the need for landfill (to reclaim land from the swamp), and "piles" (timber poles driven through the soft swampy soil onto the solid bedrock). Poor foundations have plagued recent building projects and several modern houses can be seen leaning over at precarious angles as they settle on shifting swampland.

The Maya Mountains

The capital of Belize, Belmopan, is at the foothills of the Maya Mountains. It is a new city born out of the devastation caused to Belize City in 1961 by Hurricane Hattie. Belize's government and much of the diplomatic service relocated to Belmopan following Hattie, but most others chose to stay put. Belmopan remains a quiet, well laid-out community, but it lacks Belize City's lively Caribbean character. It contains a dreary collection of government buildings that are supposed to be arranged in the style of a Mayan plaza – part of George Price's romantic Mayan ideal that was lost somewhere between the vision and the work of the British architect who designed it.

The atmosphere and culture in this part of Belize, the Cayo District, is Hispanic for the same reason as that found in the northern districts of Corozal and Orange Walk – immigration. But the immigration in this area is more recent. Since the 1980s as many as 40,000 Guatemalans, Hondurans, and Salvadorans have entered Belize, fleeing war and seeking economic opportunity. Many entered through the western border close to San Ignacio and settled in and around the Cayo area. Others traveled south to seek work in the citrus and banana industries, while some sought employment in the sugar industry in the north of the country. This number is reinforced by continued immigration that has made Spanish probably more widely spoken here than English, though most people are bi-lingual.

The west is the destination for most of Belize's inland tourists because of its developed tourist infrastructure and beautiful scenery. Although most destinations are at the foothills of the Maya Mountains, areas higher up into the mountains are being opened up, mainly to tourism and archeological and forest research facilities. The excavations at the Caracol Maya site (which is now recognized as one of the most important cities in the Maya region) and the consequent improvement of the road to this site deep in the Mountain Pine Ridge, have made the area gradually more accessible. Some of Belize's premier tourist resorts, including Francis Ford Coppola's Blancaneaux Lodge, are in the Mountain Pine Ridge. Despite the development that has taken place, the region is still mainly unspoiled, and includes vast tracts of pristine forest, rivers and waterfalls, and extensive, little-explored limestone cave systems.

The Forgotten South

The south is the forgotten region of Belize, but it is also the most ethnically diverse, with Garifuna, Creole, Mopan and Ke'chi Maya, mestizo and Mennonite communities. Although government money has most often gone north and west, the south has recently been receiving more attention as new roads, electricity, and water systems are beginning to be put into the area's towns and villages. It is undoubtedly the country's most inhospitable area, with its heaviest rainfall, densest forest and worst infrastructure. A small group of American confederates attempted to establish a community in the southernmost town of Punta Gorda after the American Civil War but found the conditions too harsh. It is a testimony to the resilience of Belize's southern inhabitants that they not only have managed to survive, but have also begun developing the area into a more welcoming environment.

While the government sets about its largest single infrastructural improvement project – the paving of the Southern Highway linking Dangriga Town to the most southerly town, Punta Gorda – strong concerns have been voiced about the impact this project will have on the lives of the people involved, especially the Maya of the south. Local and foreign investors and speculators are forcing up land prices, and the traditional Mayan lands, which have poor legal protection, are under threat.

Forced by effective lobbying by Belize's Mayan community, the government and donors to the Southern Highway project have made some attempt to offset the problems associated with the road building by insisting on more consultation, and have set up an Environmental and Social Technical Assistance Project (ESTAP) to try to address the concerns of communities along the Southern Highway route. The commitment of the government and the private sector to resolving the land issue still remains a big question.

Fruit and Labor

Even as the south is beginning to develop an eco-tourism industry, with people attracted by the region's unique cultural diversity, the major economic activity in this part of the country remains citrus cultivation. Groves are planted from Cayo down to Toledo Districts, but the industry is centered on two modern processing plants a few miles outside Dangriga Town. The other main industry, banana cultivation, is smaller and more localized, based around the port town of Big Creek. Both these industries, citing the unavailability and unsuitability of local workers, have a policy of employing Central American immigrants. As a result, many new mestizo communities have grown up along the Hummingbird and Southern Highways, near the citrus processing plants and the citrus and banana plantations. These are interspersed with existing Maya and Garifuna communities.

The immigrants are also attracted to the towns in the area – the pre-dominantly Creole towns of Independence and Placencia, as well as the Garifuna towns of Dangriga and Punta Gorda – in search of work. The character of these towns is changing noticeably with the opening up of mestizo-run businesses, mainly bars and shops, and intermarriage between mestizo immigrants and locals.

Reef, Cayes and Atolls

Belize's barrier reef is probably the country's greatest national asset. It acts as a natural barrier to protect the coastline, is a breeding ground for lobster, conch and fish, and attracts tourists drawn to the unique snorkeling and diving opportunities it offers.

There are more than 200 offshore islands, referred to as "cayes" (caye being a corruption of the Spanish word *cayo* or "little island"). Most of the cayes lie along the reef itself and within the Inner Channel (the shallow – six to thirty feet deep – stretch of water between the reef and the mainland). Many of the cayes are made up almost entirely of mangrove swamp with little or no firm land. Mangroves also grow along the Belizean coast. They are a critical part of the eco-system, because their roots help stop erosion by trapping sediment and the shelter they give provides a good environment for fish to breed. The cutting down of mangroves is discouraged, and requires government permission. Despite this, the pressure for more housing and tourism development along the coast and on the cayes is causing more and more mangroves to be cleared.

While most of the larger cayes house a variety of tourist accommodation, private guest houses and research facilities, only two cater for tourism on a commercial scale. The largest and most developed is Ambergris, (named after the waxy substance found in sperm whales that was once used in making perfumes) which is the same size as the island of Barbados. Like Barbados, it has a well developed tourist industry based on the main town of San Pedro, although unlike Barbados, much of the island's land is uninhabitable mangrove swamp. Ambergris, once an important Maya trading center, forms part of a limestone peninsula that runs from the southernmost tip of Quintana Roo in Mexico, and most of its residents are mestizos of Mexican descent.

South of Ambergris Caye is the second most developed caye, Caye Caulker, which is also popular with tourists. The Spanish originally called this Hicaco, but British pirates anglicized its name to "Caulker". Caye Caulker is much smaller than Ambergris and was split in two along a channel called "The Split" by the fierce winds of Hurricane Hattie in 1961.

In addition to its reef and cayes, Belize also has three atolls: Lighthouse Reef, Glover's Reef and the Turneffe Islands. An atoll is a ring-shaped coral island that fringes an enclosed, relatively shallow lagoon. While atolls are fairly common in the Pacific and other tropical oceans, only one other such formation exists in the entire Caribbean. They are further from the mainland than the cayes, and so the waters in and around them are noticeably clearer, unaffected by the mud carried by the rivers into the sea, or from pollutants discharged from the coastal settlements.

The Living Forest

Belize's forest is of critical importance both to Belize and to the world. Not only does it provide habitat and livelihood for significant numbers of Belize's human population, but it also plays an important role in maintaining climate. Destruction of the forest is not only responsible for destroying human and animal habitat as well as unique plant life, but also can have devastating effects on the world's weather systems.

Belize's forest is one of the world's most remarkable and colorful eco-systems, hosting a wide range of animal life including jaguars and pumas, ocelots and tapirs, and a bewildering variety of birds including toucans, hawks and parrots. The forest also contains an extraordinary number of trees, plants and insects. Several animal and plant species are already threatened because of the continued destruction being inflicted on this environment in the name of progress. As deforestation continues to destroy natural habitat, other species will become endangered and some may die out altogether.

Belize's forests have played a major role in the development of the country. During the height of the Maya civilization much of the forest was cleared to support agriculture. The decline of the Maya, probably as a

Sacred Ceiba tree   *James Beveridge*

result of this deforestation, allowed the regeneration of the forest, which then became the target of European economic exploitation, first for logwood (*palo de tinte*), which was valuable as a wool dye to the British textile industry, and shortly afterwards, mahogany. Logwood was cut from the late 1660s onwards.

Mahogany was found deeper in the interior and needed more labor for extraction, so the Europeans imported African slaves from Jamaica and elsewhere in the English Caribbean in the eighteenth century. The European loggers (known as "Baymen" because they were mostly based around the Bay of Honduras) established "mahogany works" or logging camps along the main rivers. Until the introduction of mechanization in the 1940's, felled trees were hauled by oxen to the river in the dry season and in the wet season, as the rivers swelled, floated down together in "booms" to the port at Belize City. The indiscriminate logging that followed mechanization soon led to the decline of the industry as the best and most accessible trees were cleared without any thought given to replanting.

After several decades of stagnation, commercial exploitation of Belize's forests is once again on the increase. In 1995, a twenty-year logging license was issued to a Malaysian company, Atlantic Industries. This license covers 200,000 acres of the Columbia River Forest Reserve in the Toledo

District, and its award has sparked off a fierce controversy that has put a number of important issues at the forefront of public debate.

Environmentalists are concerned that since this area of the country contains Belize's only true tropical rainforest, a large-scale logging operation will have detrimental environmental consequences. Local and international environmental organizations have expressed a great deal of concern about Atlantic's presence in Belize. Although a logging plan that is supposed to ensure the sustainability of logging operations is in place, some people question the ability of Belize's Forest Department to adequately monitor Atlantic Industries. The plan stipulates that trees felled must be over a certain age and only a limited number of these mature trees can be felled within a given area. While the Forest Department has the technical expertise to monitor the plan, it has limited financial and physical resources at its disposal.

Forest Clearing and Milpa Farming

The other main issue raised by the Atlantic Industries affair concerns the rights of the Maya over the lands on which they live. The Maya who live within the Columbia River Forest Reserve have expressed their concerns that the logging will affect their traditional way of life, and that they have been excluded from the decision-making process. In response, Maya representative groups from the area have formed alliances with international environmental and indigenous peoples' groups to put pressure on the government to listen to the Maya viewpoint.

The threat to the forest comes not only from commercial exploitation by international companies such as Atlantic, or the smaller local logging firms; it also comes from the needs of agricultural activities, notably the citrus and banana industries, and the traditional farming practices of small subsistence farmers.

Thousands of acres of forest have been cleared to make way for banana and citrus plantations, and more land is continually being cleared. This will undoubtedly cause long-term damage to the already poor soils in this region of the country, as Belize's tropical rains (which are among the heaviest in the world) wash away unprotected topsoil.

Thousands more acres are being cleared by subsistence *milpa* farmers. Milpa farming is a form of slash and burn agriculture, in which farmers clear an area of forest with machetes and then burn whatever remains to create their farming plot, or milpa. The two crops usually planted in these milpas are corn and beans, while pigs are also kept and fed on any plant waste.

If well practiced, milpa farming is sustainable, as farmers move from their milpa after one or two crops, and do not return to it for many years (if at all). This gives the forest the chance to begin to recover. However sustainable milpa farming depends on the density of milpa farmers in a given area of forest. As Belize's rural population has expanded over the past twenty years, the number of subsistence farmers has increased substantially, putting ever more pressure on the forest. Monitoring the impact of this farming is probably even more difficult than monitoring commercial logging operations, as milpa farms tend to be in remote rural locations.

The Environment, Tourism and Eco-Science

Belize's major resource as a nation, after its people, is its environment. And the environment is a resource only so long as it is protected. Two factors make Belize's environment attractive to the outside world: first, it is accessible, particularly from the United States, the origin of most of the visitors to Belize (whether they are tourists, investors or researchers), and second, it is relatively unspoiled. The need to attract visitors to keep revenues flowing, while at the same time keeping the resources intact, means the Belize government is sometimes forced into a difficult balancing act.

While the government has designated about one-third of all national lands in Belize under Forest Reserves and Protected Area status, it has to find the resources to manage these areas effectively, as well as respond to pressures from commercial interests to develop protected areas, or from environmental lobbyists to extend protection.

The tourism industry, for instance, which has rapidly become an essential part of Belize's economy, needs more development if it is to expand. In particular, it requires more and better resorts and better infrastructure including air, road and sea transportation. On the other hand, development of the tourism industry needs to be managed to avoid damaging the environmental resources that attract tourists in the first place. Fortunately, it is unlikely that Belize will enter the mass tourist market, which is well catered for elsewhere in the Caribbean, Mexico and Central America. This gives the government and the industry a better chance to manage growth than if Belize were expecting the unbridled growth of major resort development.

The management of this tourism growth is assisted by the reputation Belize has earned for scientific research. Belize offers scientists relatively easy access to study some of the world's most important eco-systems: coral reef, wetlands and forests. The Belizean government and education establishments have been positively embracing relationships with overseas institutions. This has led to the creation of world-class local scientific research facilities through innovative joint initiatives with foreign research institutes, for example, with the Washington D.C.-based Smithsonian Institute and the British Natural History Museum.

Another trend is toward attracting people who are willing to pay to study and participate in research projects in this diverse eco-system. This science-based tourism looks set to give Belize another lucrative string in its tourism bow, providing much-needed income to the country and at the same time developing educational facilities which can be used by Belizean students and professionals to learn about their country and help safeguard their environment.

Facilities and projects involving international organizations operating in Belize's offshore waters include the Smithsonian's research station on Carrie Bow Caye, and the British-based Coral Caye Conservation Association, which is working with the University College of Belize to create a local marine research facility. Texas A&M University's research station is studying the behavior of bottlenose dolphins at Blackbird Caye in the Turneffe Islands, where it is possible for visitors to participate in studies.

Inland, the Las Cuevas Research Station in the Chiquibul forest, deep inside the Mountain Pine Ridge, is a research facility established under a joint initiative between the government of Belize and the Natural History Museum, London. The research station hosts teams of scientists, mainly from the UK, who have the chance to study this previously little explored environment.

Local Initiatives

The two most prominent local organizations involved in conservation efforts are the Belize Audubon Society (BAS) and Programme for Belize (PFB). BAS is the caretaker of the Half Moon Caye Natural Monument, found on Lighthouse Reef. This 10,000-acre atoll, together with the fifteen square miles of surrounding waters, was the first area designated under the 1981 National Parks Systems and Wildlife Protection Acts. It protects a 4,000-strong red-footed booby colony and is home to a further 98 bird species. The only other such red-footed booby colony in the Caribbean is on Tobago Island off the Venezuelan coast. The BAS is also involved in managing several of Belize's inland environmental resources, including Tapir Mountain Nature Reserve, Guanacaste National Park and Blue Hole National Park. PFB manages the 228,000-acre Rio Bravo Conservation and Management Area.

Organizations such as the BAS and PFB are finding it increasingly difficult to attract funding for their work. This brings the long-term sustainability of such operations into question unless they are able to generate their own income. It is also important that such initiatives are able to create environmentally sustainable economic opportunities for people living in protected areas.

Natural Devastation

The environment can also throw up its own destructive forces, the most damaging of which in the Caribbean region are hurricanes. Despite sophisticated early warning systems, millions of dollars of damage is caused almost every year in the Caribbean by these ferocious storms. Winds can gust at speeds of over 180 miles per hour, bringing down power lines, trees and buildings and whipping the sea into a frenzy.

Hurricanes have caused enormous destruction in Belize over the years. On September 10, 1931, a major hurricane hit Belize City, causing extensive loss of life and property damage. In 1955 Hurricane Janet (by then hurricanes were given names to assist with tracking), caused similar damage to Corozal Town in the north of the country. The last major hurricane to strike was Hurricane Hattie, which devastated Belize City and Dangriga on October 31, 1961. Hattie claimed hundreds of lives and caused millions of dollars in property damage. In October 1998 Hurricane Mitch caused hundreds of deaths in Nicaragua and Honduras, but Belize was less seriously affected. Nevertheless, the hurricane's threatened arrival led to a full-scale evacuation of tourists and other precautionary measures.

"Tourists Take No Chances"

As Belizeans called relatives inland to arrange temporary housing or contemplated going to shelters, many of the visitors to our shores – and even nearby waters – opted to try and catch a plane home. Needless to say, the Philip S.W. Goldson International Airport was packed by an anxious, but patient crowd. News Five was there.

As the evacuation was carried out today on the islands of San Pedro Ambergris Caye and Caye Caulker, the Philip Goldson International Airport was filled to capacity as tourist after tourist lined up to catch next available flight out to the United States. According to a Tropic Air spokesperson, between six a.m. and twelve thirty p.m., they flew out five to six hundred tourists.

Tourist#1

"We arrived here about six thirty."

Q: "What is the atmosphere like out there on the island?"

Tourist#1

"It was really pretty calm; it was really pretty calm. It was really confused at the beginning, but things worked out by the middle of the morning."

Q: "Were a lot of people evacuating from the island?"

Tourist#1

"There were still quite a number of people on the street."

Tourist#2

Hurricane Mitch "missed" Belize, but still had the power to topple buildings.

James Beveridge

"We've been here a week. We had intended to stay a bit longer, however, and we were looking at property to buy and develop."

Q: "We understand the evacuation started this morning. How did the island look this morning? A lot of people leaving?"

Tourist#2

"A lot of people leaving. Locals closing up yesterday and fairly orderly; a little panic."

Also trying to catch a flight out to the U.S. were ninety-seven passengers who were shipped in from off the coast of Honduras, after their ride on the Windjammer cruise got interrupted by Hurricane Mitch.

Tourist#3

"We came off of the S.V. Phantome, off Honduras and they are evacuating everybody to Miami. We just came off from the ship."

Tourist#4

"We left San Pedro Sula last night. Actually, I was here all night long. We went out and couldn't get around the storm, so they brought us into Belize City to fly. So they are taking the ship out to sea to ride the storm out."

While at this time we do not know if Hurricane Mitch will have a devastating effect on Belize, some residents in the city were not wasting any time in preparing for the powerful storm. We observed many people buying timber and boarding up their houses; even the employees at the international airport were securing and boarding up the glass windows.

Belize's Channel 5 News, October 1998, reporting on the threatened strike of Hurricane Mitch

2   HISTORY AND POLITICS: FROM ENCLAVE TO NATIONHOOD

Early Civilization

The Ancient Maya civilization is usually divided into three periods: Pre-Classic (1200 BC to 250 AD), Classic (250 to 900 AD) and Post-Classic (900 to 1508 AD). The Maya lived throughout Central America in what is now southern Mexico, El Salvador, western Honduras, Belize, and Guatemala. They had no centralized political system, and lived in distinct city-states that engaged in both trade and war between themselves. They were also influenced by contact with other indigenous groups, especially to the north in Mexico.

While Europeans came to Belize in search of short-term wealth to enrich their home countries, for the Maya, this was home. Long before the Europeans came, the Maya had established sophisticated trading relationships over a wide area including the Caribbean, Mexico and Central America. And they had made remarkable achievements in architecture, astronomy, mathematics, writing and the arts.

The arrival of the Europeans had a devastating effect on the Central American Maya, but the real collapse of Maya civilization had occurred at least 600 years earlier. Since the height of its power in 900 AD, the Maya civilization had begun to transform itself, affected by overpopulation and/or changing environmental conditions. Historians estimate that Belize's Maya population at the time of the first European contact had fallen from over one million to about 200,000, very much the same as Belize's present day population.

The Arrival of the Europeans

The first Spanish contact with the Maya of Belize came in the early 1500s when exploratory Spanish fleets sailing along Central America's coastline came into contact with coastal Mayan villages. This began the long period of suffering that the Maya were to endure at the hands of the Europeans.

The Spanish did not give the Belize region high priority, although Spanish religious and military expeditions regularly passed through Maya territory and some attempts were made to administer the territory from Mexico. Spanish priests introduced Catholicism, converting whole villages and replacing Maya symbols of worship with Christian ones. Some villages were "rationalized"; that is, moved to central locations to be more easily administered. There are also reports of atrocities committed by Spanish expeditionary forces against the Maya, and of both Spanish and British

Maya Caracol site   *James Beveridge*

pirates taking Maya captive for slaves. The British employed Mesquito Indians from the Nicaraguan coast to aid them in the slave trade. The Maya continued to resist, burning Christian churches and fighting back against their attackers.

By the time the British settlers began their logging activities in the seventeenth century, Belize's Maya population had been devastated. Nevertheless, they continued to put up strong resistance against encroachment on their lands. It was only with the assistance of military reinforce-ments sent from Jamaica that the settlers were eventually, by the end of the nineteenth century, able to subdue Maya resistance.

Central American Backwater

The Spanish invaders of the sixteenth century found Belize an inhospitable territory; navigating its coastal waters through the barrier reef was a treacherous affair, and the marshy swamp and dense jungle of the inland were not any easier to penetrate. Central America was regarded as the backwater of the Spanish Americas, and the territory of Belize was the backwater of the backwaters. It had little of the type of natural resources sought by the Spaniards, but they nevertheless staked their claim.

Further European conquest was left to British buccaneers, who had discovered the channels through the reef, enabling them to maneuver their ships in and out of Belize's coastal waters. They used the reef's shelter to attack and plunder Spanish vessels, and gradually, in the mid-1600s, began to settle.

After the 1670 Treaty of Madrid committed the British to suppress piracy, the settlers sought other economic opportunities. The trade that was to be the basis for the development of Belize was timber – firstly logwood, which grew nearer the coast, and then mahogany, which was found further inland. The British "Baymen," as they called themselves, along with African slaves shipped from Jamaica, made their first main settlement on St. George's Caye, a small island a few miles off the coast of Belize. This was succeeded by a more conveniently located settlement at the mouth of the Belize River, which was to develop into Belize City, today's commercial capital.

At the request of the British government, Spain agreed to give the settlers logging rights in three separate agreements in 1763, 1783 and 1786. The final agreement called for the British to relocate more than 2,000 settlers from the Mosquito Shore on the Nicaraguan/Honduran coast to Belize. Despite the agreements, Spanish forces continued to launch attacks on the British settlers, culminating in the Battle of St. George's Caye on September 10, 1798. This relatively minor sea battle established the British as the superior military power in the area, and Spain acknowledged British sovereignty over Belize in the 1802 Treaty of Amiens. The Battle of St. George's Caye is now celebrated every year, especially by more conservative Creole Belizeans who see it as a unifying event, in which settlers and slaves fought side by side for their country. Others see it as having little or no significance to modern Belize. They argue that it was a colonial battle, in which slaves were forced against their will into the front lines of the confrontation.

The Early Economy

The early economy was dominated by a forestry industry that became increasingly concentrated in the hands of a few companies. By the mid-nineteenth century the main companies were Young, Toledo and Company, and James Hyde and Company. James Hyde and Co. became the British Honduras Company in 1860 and then the Belize Estate and Produce Company (BEC) in 1875. BEC absorbed Young, Toledo and Co. in 1880. Based at Hill Bank, the BEC came to exert enormous influence on Belize, since it owned huge swathes of land that included the best mahogany and Mexican cedar trees.

The other commercial forest-based economic activity was the production of chicle, a gum extracted from the trunk of the sapodilla tree and used in the manufacture of chewing gum. Chicle harvesting reached its peak in 1939, when it was the second most important Belizean export after mahogany. Synthetic substitutes developed in the 1950s led to a reduction in the trade, although there has been a resurgence in recent years, with Japan a particularly lucrative market.

The trade was based on concessions that were subcontracted to *chiclero* gangs who operated from camps in the forest during the wet season. Most chicleros were Mayan or Waika Indians who had come from the Mosquito Coast. Since the chiclero gangs operated so deep in the forest, they, along with the Maya, were the people who best knew the interior of the country; in fact, many of the Maya archeological sites in Belize were first re-discovered by the chicleros.

Once harvested, the chicle was boiled down into 22-lb. blocks and sold to the concessionaire. The industry operated with little control and in the northern forests, all sapodilla trees, the source of the best chicle, and virtually every *chicle macho* tree, which produces poorer quality gum, still carry tapping scars. Many other latex-producing trees also carry scars as chicleros used to add this latex to the chicle to make up their blocks. Indiscriminate tapping meant that the northern forests were soon overworked, and it did not pay to transfer activity to the south of the country where quality was poor and transport costs high, so eventually the chicleros travelled further, into Mexico and Guatemala, bringing what they harvested or bought from the local chiclero gangs back into Belize for sale in the U.S. and British market.

In 1935, forest products accounted for 82.2 percent of all exports, and 97 percent of these forest products consisted of mahogany, cedar and chicle. But the logging industry was far from stable or efficient and with prices and demand fluctuating wildly, the poorly managed industry in Belize struggled to survive.

The logging and chicle industries suffered rapid decline in the early to mid-twentieth century as timber supplies dried up, and, in the case of chicle, synthetic substitutes were discovered. The decline of the industry was due in large part to bad management of forest resources. As the industrial age gave the loggers more tools with which to extract timber, extraction rates increased dramatically, and within a short time, the number of workable sites decreased equally dramatically.

Colonial Economic Policy

The colonial administration was anxious to diversify the economy, mindful of the dangers of mono-culturism. Yet all good land was in the hands of the "forestocracy," who effectively controlled the legislature and finances of the colony, along with a small number of merchants who controlled the colony's imports and exports. These people did what they could to avoid paying taxes, and public expenditures were kept to what could be covered by revenues from import and export duties.

During the first three decades of the twentieth century, the colony was in sound financial shape. Until the First World War, revenues and expenditure had balanced at around $500,000 per annum, while during the war itself the increased price paid for timber increased annual revenues to over $1 million. Low taxes meant, however, that, despite sound finance, the settlers effectively restricted the colony's development by not investing in roads, port facilities, or social services such as education and health.

Attempts to diversify revenue collection away from export and import duties failed. A land tax introduced in 1871 provided minimal income as the settlers more often than not avoided payment. An income tax introduced in 1920 was also very lenient toward those in the upper-income bracket and yielded little income, and it was not until the mid-1940s that income tax generated any significant revenue. In 1945, $221,175 was collected, with 57 percent of this coming from three individuals and five companies.

Because the colony was so reliant on trade, the Great Depression of the 1930s had a devastating effecton its economy. Imports halved from $5 million in 1930 to $2 million in 1933, with exports experiencing a similar drop. The hurricane that struck Belize City in 1931 was the final straw, and the local legislature relinquished control of the finances to the Imperial Treasury.

Some trading houses used this time to consolidate their position. Whisky smuggling into the Prohibition-bound U.S. became a major export activity with re-exports of whisky rising from 1,436 gallons worth $6,040 in 1921 to 217,577 gallons worth $1.1 million in 1931.

The local businessmen had a vested interest in protecting the dominance of the forestry industry. They wanted among other things to protect their import business, which would be threatened by diversified local production and manufacturing. Nevertheless, despite the resistance of the forestocracy, the colonial government successfully diversified production into sugar and citrus, giving both of these crops preferential access into the UK market.

For the first time in 1959, citrus and banana exports together surpassed forestry exports, signaling the beginning of the end of the forestry industry's domination of Belize life. There were some attempts to diversify timber production into pine in the 1950s, but as with previous forestry activities, within a few short years accessible supplies were quickly depleted, and it was not cost-effective to travel the long distances needed to reach the remaining trees. The industry therefore lost out to cheaper Nicaraguan pine.

Land

Only an estimated 19 percent of Belize's land is capable of supporting agriculture without heavy investment in drainage, fertilizers and soil retention, but a significant portion of this best land remains uncultivated in large foreign-owned estates.

The settlers' methods for distributing land were initially based on what was needed for the logwood, and then mahogany, trade. They devised a system for allocating each settler areas of land, known as "works," next to a river (which was the only means of transportation), with restrictions on the size and number of such holdings. As the settlement became more permanent, they declared these lands to be "deemed at law to be freehold property" of the occupants.

In 1820 this system of ownership by occupancy was abolished, except for existing holdings, and the remaining land was deemed to be Crown Land. This land was given out in free grants, which were popular until the introduction of a land fee in 1839. As Crown Land consisted largely of poorer lands in the less accessible south of the country, the settlers were unwilling to pay the fee and the distribution of Crown Lands slowed down considerably. In order to formalize the recording of land ownership, the colonial administration introduced the Land Registry in 1859, and between 1859 and 1864 nearly all logwood and mahogany works were registered.

By the late nineteenth century, some 2,500,000 acres of land, the best land in the country, was held in freehold by the forestocracy. 96 owners held 97 percent of this land (including BEC with one million acres), while 1,552 owners shared the other three percent. The three million remaining acres was Crown Land.

As the forestry industry declined, the mostly absentee landowners did not invest in their estates because they had become used to earning large profits with minimal investment. Most of the mahogany profits were invested abroad, mainly in the U.S. The landowners resisted selling their lands, opting instead to wait and see whether land prices would rise. The newly elected government introduced a Land Tax Law in 1966 in an attempt to move the land market, but landowners responded by laying off workers and selling off small parcels of land, or leasing land out to milpa′ farmers, using the collective rents to pay the tax.

The introduction of the Alien Land Holdings Act in 1973 put some restrictions on the further diminution of available land through foreign ownership, but lack of access to productive land has remained a severe constraint on agricultural development. Improvements being made to roads, especially in the south, have opened up access to previously worthless tracts of government-owned land, but this has also introduced the new problem of subsistence farmers having to compete for land with plantations and speculators.

Labor and Unemployment

For much of the colony's early history, labor was in short supply, and after the abolition of slavery the forestry industry guarded its workforce through a combination of keeping workers in debt, strict labor laws and a work ethic that favored forestry over agricultural production. Forestry workers were usually hired in Belize City at Christmas on eleven-month contracts starting in January, when they would set up their work camps along the rivers deep into the forest. Even when demand for lumber fell, workers were guaranteed work, although their working conditions left a lot to be desired.

By the beginning of the First World War in 1914, the colony's first unemployment was registered, although many subsequently found war-related employment, including service in the army. After the war, however, the unemployment problem remained, and was compounded first by the Depression and then by the 1931 hurricane. Some work was found in the construction industry following the hurricane, but this was short-lived.

The colonial government started up welfare programs and the situation was so bad that food depots were set up in Belize City to feed the poor. Some people left to find work on the banana plantations of the neighboring republics, but this route closed in 1939 when these countries took steps to protect their indigenous labor force.

The introduction in the 1930s and 1940s of mechanized transport in the logging industry improved flexibility and output, but also cost many workers their jobs as new short-term contracts were introduced and the industry's decline was hastened by overproduction. War once again helped the unemployment problem, as men were needed to work in the U.S., UK and in the Panama Canal Zone during the Second World War. But as before, the end of the war signaled the return to unemployment in Belize for most of these workers.

While the forestocracy did little or nothing to aid the labor situation, the colonial government made efforts to push for improvements in working conditions in the colony. This led to the legalizing of trade unionism in 1941, and the repeal of the Masters and Servants Ordinance of 1883 and the Fraudulent Labourers Ordinance of 1922. This gave a legal basis to the organized labor movement, which had grown out of rising unemployment and poverty.

Trade unions in Belize prospered during the 1950s and 1960s, under the pro-labor People's United Party (PUP). Although they were successful in promoting better working conditions, they were weakened by the ready availability of immigrant labor, a vulnerable economy, poor organization, and infighting. In today's Belize, trade unionism is in crisis, and the much needed improvements in labor rights and conditions require concerted effort by government, local and regional trade unions, the private sector and human rights organizations.

Politics and Democracy

The fact that the Spanish claimed sovereignty over the territory until 1802, and Britain recognized this claim, meant that the first British colonists were slow to exercise political or legal authority over the settlement. The settlers were left in a precarious position, at odds with the Spanish and the local Maya inhabitants, and also very often with each other. A growing number of internal disputes led the settlers to start to develop their own set of rules and regulations, mainly to do with logging rights. After the 1763 Treaty of Paris between Britain and Spain, the first attempts were made to formalize political authority. In 1765, Admiral Sir William Burnaby, Commander-in-Chief of the British naval squadron in Jamaica, wrote a primitive constitution based on the settlers' existing rules, which came to be known as "Burnaby's Code."

The first form of government in Belize was the "Public Meeting," which set the territory's laws and elected magistrates who exercised judicial and administrative functions. A small number of wealthy settlers controlled this system, which was based on wealth and color. In 1787, when the first British-appointed administrator, the "Superintendent," arrived to represent British interests in the newly named "British Honduras," twelve settlers owned four-fifths of the land.

The settlers welcomed the first Superintendent, Colonel Edward Marcus Despard, because of his military credentials. But after the Battle of St. George's Caye, the Superintendent's growing involvement in civilian affairs was not so welcome. There followed a period of uneasy relations, with the Superintendent often at odds with the settlers, and the British government not particularly keen to take sides.

Belize Becomes a Colony

The Public Meeting gradually lost its power as the mahogany trade slumped and the forestocracy became indebted to London-based merchants. Following the 1838 abolition of slavery, non-whites began to have increasing influence in the political arena; "free coloreds" who were the offspring of liaisons between whites and their black slaves gradually began to gain political and economic power.

Attempting to wrest power away from the Superintendent, the settlers pushed for an elected Legislative Assembly, which Britain approved in 1853, as part of the first formal constitution. Constant disagreements in the Assembly, however, resulted in the settlers voting for it to be replaced by a nominated Legislative Council and an Executive Council in which a British-appointed "Governor" would have the decisive vote. This system, begun in 1871, marked the beginning of Belize's status as an official British Crown Colony.

The Governor's use of the casting vote in 1890 had dramatic effects, as five members resigned from the Executive Council in protest and formed the People's Committee (PC), Belize's first modern political organization. The PC aimed to "redeem the country's political inheritance from the temporary custodian." Local businesses refused to recognize the legality of the Legislative Council's proclamations, and nobody from the colony would agree to serve as a member unless they were guaranteed a majority. The Governor, on the advice of the British government, eventually agreed to this in 1892. This system, which was to last until 1954, was dominated by the BEC.

Winds of Change

The ruling elite, the landowners and merchants, exercised tremendous power in the colony, doing everything in their power to prevent the rise of the nouveaux riches, mainly free coloreds and mestizos, who were growing in influence and number. Nevertheless, after the First World War, as hundreds of disbanded soldiers and unemployed rioted at the poor treatment they received from the colonial government, it became clear that a more open political system was needed. The 1931 hurricane and Great Depression exacerbated the colony's problems, as did a fire in Belize City in 1933, which was followed the same year by one of the worst floods ever along the Belize River.

Despite the hardships, there was no concerted mass political action during the 1930s, perhaps because Belize lacked an industrial center and an organized workers' movement. The boost given to employment and the economy by the Second World War may have postponed the emergence of the nationalist movement. It may, on the other hand, even have quickened the pace as Belizeans travelling abroad to work in the U.S., UK and Panama, met with others engaged in similar struggles. After the war, economic hardships remained, unemployment was high and the stage was set for fundamental change.

The rise of nationalist politics in Belize in the 1940s mirrored the same general response to British colonial rule that was seen throughout the Caribbean and elsewhere, although the reaction in the 1930s to rising economic hardships was less dramatic than in other Caribbean territories. The 1935 disturbance by the Unemployed Workers' Association, headed somewhat reluctantly by Antonio Soberanis, was the most memorable of the several demonstrations around this time, including strikes and boycotts. The lack of mass movements can be partly explained by the nature of employment in Belize, which saw workers spread throughout the country on dispersed forestry work sites for eleven months of the year. Communication and organization were therefore extremely difficult.

In September 1949, the UK revalued the £ sterling. A consequent devaluation of the British Honduras Dollar (BH$) was rejected by the Legislative Council, but the Governor, Sir Ronald Garvey, used his reserve power to force through a devaluation in December of the same year. This was the event to galvanize the nationalist movement. It succeeded in uniting the local business elite with emerging young radical politicians against the colonial regime.

Several organizations and institutions were involved in fomenting the nationalist movement. The Open Forum held in Battlefield Park, was an informal debating society that attracted seasoned political campaigners and those whose political awareness had awakened during the Second World War. Its Chairman, Ethelbert "Kid" Broaster, had been deported from the U.S. after advocating non-participation of American blacks in the war.

The General Workers' Union (GWU), which covered several occupational groups, saw its membership spiral from 350 in 1943 to 3,000 in 1948. The GWU was the only mass membership organization with roots in the districts, achieved through its struggles with the BEC and colonial government to make contact with and represent workers. The *Belize Billboard* newspaper, founded in 1946 by a Cuban national, Narciso Valdés, spoke out for the working classes and championed the cause of the GWU.

The organization from which Belize's early political leaders were to emerge was the Christian Social Action Group (CSAG), formed by graduates of Belize's foremost secondary educational establishment, the Jesuit-run St. John's College. These Catholic young men, brought up under the liberal religious and political teachings of the Jesuits, had forged a solidarity that went beyond cultural and ethnic divisions.

That these new political leaders of the country were Catholics indicates that rather than there being political conflict along ethnic lines (as in Guyana or Trinidad), Belize's political battle lines were drawn between

Catholics and Protestants. Catholics tended to be more ethnically diverse, spread throughout the country and more representative of the lower classes, while Protestants were almost solely Belize City Creoles who were closer to the ruling colonial authorities.

The People's United Party

In January 1950, the People's Committee (PC) was re-formed with the aim of ending colonial rule. Mass support was immediately forthcoming because of the poor living conditions of the majority of the people in the colony. In the same year the PC evolved into the People's United Party (PUP) and its leaders orchestrated the take-over of the GWU at its seventh annual conference, giving them a national mass support base. In both its appeal to the poor majority and its nationalist ideology, the party was similar to other newly created organizations across the region. The founding of the PUP came in the same year that the People's Progressive Party was formed in Guyana, and six years earlier than the People's National Movement in Trinidad.

The emergent leader of the PUP, George Price, took a very pro-U.S. line during its campaigning, arguing that the U.S. and not the UK was the natural trading partner of Belize. Price was probably influenced by his close relationship with his employer, R.S. Turton, the Belizean multi-millionaire who had extensive business connections in the U.S. and large shareholdings in two U.S. companies, the Wrigley Co., and I.T. Williams Co., rivals to BEC in chicle and mahogany production respectively. Turton, despite his vast wealth, was outside the elite of Belize society. He was a staunch critic of the government and had lost heavily in the devaluation.

In an attempt to bolster relations after the devaluation, the Governor announced the visit of Princess Alice in 1950. This highlighted some of the differences of opinion within the PUP. "God Bless America" had been adopted as the people's song at party rallies, and Price wanted this sung during the visit of the Princess. "Kid" Broaster, for his part, objected because of the treatment he had seen blacks receiving in the U.S. As a result, he was turned on by Price and the crowds, and needed police protection. Because of the threats of protests, the Princess' visit was cancelled.

Politics and Propaganda

A second party, the National Party (NP), was formed in August 1951 by the more socially and professionally established Creole elite of Belize City. This party represented the existing social order and sought to achieve decolonization while protecting the wealthy minority's own interests.

Price's mass popularity, positive relationship with Guatemala and anti-British stance caused the colonial government the most concern, and its

George Price in 1957   *Hulton Getty*

members sought to attack the PUP while exploiting the differences within its leadership. The government's own reform process, a Belizean Commission of Inquiry on Constitutional Reform, which reported in 1952, resulted in the introduction of universal adult suffrage in 1954, although the Executive Council, and therefore the running of the colony, was still to be under effective British control.

The government kept up its attacks on the PUP right up until the 1954 elections, boycotting the *Belize Billboard*, imprisoning its editors for 18 months on charges of sedition, and launching a judicial inquiry into Price's relationship with Guatemala. In 1951, Britain also recruited a public relations officer for Belize whose activities included counter-intelligence. The British had become increasingly worried that the PUP-Guatemala connection would shift nationalist politics to the left since the reforming Colonel Jacobo Arbenz became president of Guatemala in 1951, and expropriated the lands of the United Fruit Company in 1952.

Self-Government and Beyond

On April 28, 1954, 70 percent of the registered electorate voted in the country's first election by universal adult suffrage. The PUP won eight of the nine seats, receiving 65 percent of the total votes cast. While others in the PUP fully participated with the colonial administration in the belief that this was the best way to achieve political, economic and social progress, Price was unwilling to work within the British colonial system.

Even after he was made redundant following Turton's death in 1955, Price still refused to serve full-time in the government, instead concentrating on developing his mass popularity throughout the country. Price, who had studied for the priesthood in Guatemala, was able to win support from many who were otherwise uneasy about his apparent leanings toward the neighboring country. His charisma and nationalist ambitions, together with his mixed Creole and Mayan parentage, meant that he was able to appeal to a wide cross-section of the voting public.

Price's domination of the PUP caused a split in September 1956, with two of its Creole members leaving to form the Honduran Independence Party (HIP). The 1957 election was contested by the PUP, the HIP and the NP, and the PUP won all nine seats, although the turnout in 1957 was only 53 percent, as the PUP's political dominance led to apathy at the ballot box.

The relationship between the British government and Price continued to be tense, especially as Price appeared to be pursuing his own secret negotiations in Guatemala. Soon after the election victory, Price's contacts with Guatemalan government officials during a visit of Executive Council members to London led to his being sent home, dismissed from the Executive Council and publicly rebuked by the Governor in the Legislative Assembly and on radio. The Governor went so far as to summon a British frigate, HMS Ulster, from Jamaica in a show of strength.

In 1958 the two opposition parties merged to form the National Independence Party (NIP), and Price began to recognize that he could not achieve his goals alone despite the PUP's undoubted mass appeal. In 1959 the colonial government launched separate constitutional and economic commissions.

The commissions rejected calls for internal self-government and saw no hope of Belize developing economically unless the population was significantly increased to a sustainable 300,000 by 1975. In their opposition to these reports, Belize's political parties formed a United Front to put Belize's response to a conference with the British government in London. The conference, which began in February 1960 and lasted for seventeen days, was a turning-point in Belizean politics with the British government acceding to the United Front's proposals to bring in self-government.

After the conference, the PUP began to prepare for internal self-government, which was to take place following the 1965 elections. The British maintained control over foreign policy and security issues because of the Guatemala claim. The inexorable rise of the PUP, meanwhile, coincided with reduced British political involvement in the region, especially after the collapse of the West Indies Federation in 1961. In the 1960s, the PUP's success was staggering: in 1961 the party won all eighteen seats, in 1965 it won sixteen out of eighteen and in 1969 it took seventeen of the eighteen. It was not until 1974 that anything like an effective opposition emerged and the PUP's parliamentary strength was reduced to twelve.

Campaign headquarters of George Price, first Prime Minister of Belize   *James Beveridge*

Despite its spectacular electoral successes during these years, PUP sup-port among urban Creoles, and also in some mestizo towns, was beginning to fade. The major problem faced by the PUP was the colony's vulnerable economy, and its passive economic policy was increasingly criticized. The hoped-for U.S. investment was not forthcoming, while most of the U.S. finance entering the country was solely for the purposes of land specula-tion. The business community believed that the PUP should play a more active role in promoting foreign investment in the economy. The Cham-ber of Commerce abandoned its neutrality and became a fervent political force, launching the *Reporter* newspaper in 1966. Two of its members, Harry Lawrence and Paul Rodrigues went on to form the Liberal Party (LP) in 1973.

A New Era?

In 1968, the simultaneous return to Belize of three university graduates – Said Musa, Assad Shoman, and Evan Hyde – was the start of a potential new era in Belizean politics. All three were radical in their outlook, rejecting the comfortable status quo that appeared to characterize the political scene on their return. Having witnessed the black power movement in the U.S. and sensing the growing feeling of disenchantment among poor black youths in Belize, Hyde created the United Black Association for Development (UBAD). In the slum areas of Belize City, UBAD launched community-based programs aimed at raising awareness, providing a sense of dignity and hope, and creating employment opportunities.

In 1969 Musa and Shoman, who were both from Palestinian Arab families, formed the radical People's Action Committee (PAC), although both went on to become government ministers in the PUP. At the opposite end of the political spectrum were the ultra-conservative Creoles who formed Civic – Citizens Interested to Voice the Concerns of Country – to oppose any agreement with Guatemala. The role of Civic was unclear as the NIP had also limited itself very much to the same issue. Growing discontent among NIP members at the party's ineffectiveness culminated in the formation of the People's Democratic Movement (PDM) by a breakaway NIP member, Dean Lindo.

In late 1973 the main opposition parties – the NIP, LP and PDM – combined to form the United Democratic Party (UDP). The UDP achieved significant success against the PUP in the 1974 elections, winning six of the 19 seats. Dean Lindo, whose candidates fared best in the elections, emerged as the party's first leader. After so many years of ineffective opposition, the UDP had managed, with the support of the Belize business community, to establish itself as the only effective opposition to the PUP.

Belizean Independence and the "Guatemala Issue"

With the PUP and UDP now established as the main political forces in Belize, the 1970s was dominated by the struggle for independence. This, in turn, was enmeshed with the unresolved "Guatemalan issue" which was responsible for what Shoman called "'the Harrier mentality': the total dependence on Britain for defence translating into a dependency syndrome affecting all aspects of political life."

Guatemala's claim on Belize began after the break-up, in 1839, of the "United Provinces of Central America" into the countries of Guatemala, Honduras, El Salvador, Nicaragua and Costa Rica. Until 1823, these territories had comprised the Spanish-administered Captaincy General of Guatemala.

In 1859 the Anglo-Guatemalan Treaty, an early attempt to resolve the dispute, called on Britain and Guatemala to establish "the easiest communication (either by means of a cart-road, or employing the rivers, or both united, according to the opinion of the surveying engineers), between the fittest place on the Atlantic Coast, near the Settlement of Belize, and the capital of Guatemala."

As no road was ever built, Guatemala claimed the treaty was void, and in 1945 declared Belize its own. Modern negotiations began in 1962, and the issue was given to the U.S. to mediate. The resulting Webster proposals were an attempt by the U.S. to broker an agreement between Guatemala and Belize, but the Belizean negotiators refused to accept Webster's suggestion of an "independence of sorts," which gave neither side what they wanted—Belize, its independence, and Guatemala, seemingly, Belize. As the U.S. was more interested in developing anti-communist alliances in Guatemala than in helping Belize gain independence, its classic compromise solution did not meet Belize's aspirations, and negotiations broke down.

An international campaign by Belize resulted in the 1980 UN resolution calling for Belize's secure independence by the end of 1981 with all its territory intact, and in 1981, Belize and Guatemala signed Britain's "Heads of Agreement" document, which set out areas for future negotiation. A subsequent conference in London established Belize's post-independence constitution.

On July 26, 1981 it was announced that Belize would become independent two months later, with Britain agreeing to provide security for the new nation. The PUP team of Price, Musa and Shoman had all played key roles in winning this independence even though only a few years later the party was to lose the 1984 elections to the UDP, who had gained credibility under the guidance of Manuel Esquivel, a former secondary school physics teacher who was catapulted into his leadership role by key figures in Belize's business community.

Although the UDP was to lose the next election, the PUP's stranglehold on Belize was broken. Meanwhile, the process of democratization in Guatemala brought into power Jorge Serrano's civilian government, which finally, in 1991 recognized the independent state of Belize and established diplomatic relations. In response, Belize passed the 1992 Maritime Areas Act which limited Belize's territorial waters in the Southern Toledo area to three miles, in recognition of Guatemala's desire to have access to the Caribbean Sea.

The Guatemala issue dominated Belize's 1993 elections, especially as Britain chose that year to announce the withdrawal of its military presence. The UDP played up to growing public hysteria about the economic and political effects of the troop withdrawal and won the elections by the narrowest of margins. Adding to the equation was the new Guatemalan government's reluctance to confirm recognition of Belize. But despite a cooling of relationships immediately following the elections, Belize appointed an ambassador to Guatemala in 1997, and discussions about resuming negotiations have begun again.

Modern Belizean Politics

That there is little difference between the centrist policies of both the PUP and UDP may be why so much political campaigning is characterized by increasingly personal and vindictive attacks on key party figures. After becoming leader of the PUP following Price's retirement in 1996, Said Musa was under constant personal attack from the UDP's party newspaper, the *People's Pulse*, until the paper closed amid huge debts in late 1998, while a former UDP minister claimed that, as "an Arab, " he was not fit to be prime minister. The PUP's *Belize Times* is not far behind in its vitriolic personal attacks on leading UDP figures. The following extract from the *Belize Times* gives a flavor of the country's knockabout politics.

Esquivel No Match For Musa

"After dodging for nine months, Manuel Esquivel, former high school physics teacher and now a wealthy Prime Minister, last Thursday could find no more excuses and finally agreed to a debate/discussion with PUP Leader Said Musa on Love FM.

The debate started off on a high note about the economy but after the first segment of 20 minutes, PM Esquivel lost his wits, becoming quarrelsome, argumentative and constantly interrupting Mr Musa. In the end Mr Musa was the statesman, eloquent in his vision for Belize in the next five years and beyond. Esquivel was caught in a time warp somewhere in the 1970s and 1980s.

Musa was brilliant on his vision of the economy and of growth economics as the engine to drive Belize into the 21st century. Unable to rely on his party's performance between 1993-98, Mr Esquivel attempted to take listeners back to decades past. For Esquivel it was 'been there, done that.'

Unable to justify the long list of taxes that he had imposed, the PM sneeringly turned up his nose at two of the biggest investors in Belize, Michael Ashcroft and Barry Bowen. The PM then tooted his horn about an IMF statement in June which predicted that devaluation was a real possibility and exposed Esquivel's intention to impose new taxes on education, health and water.

Esquivel was at his weakest in health, education, and the justice system. When he was taken to task about his obvious distortions about the health system, the PM conceded that all was not well and while he was studying the situation, health care was declining. The PUP leader pledged to focus on primary health care which has collapsed under the UDP, to de-politicize the administration of the Karl Heusner Memorial Hospital and make health care available and affordable.

On education, the PUP exposed the UDP lie of 'free education' which instead made education unaffordable. While Esquivel had no plan for the future, Mr Musa spoke of 1,000 new classrooms to be built, more evening programmes, skills training, CET in every district, new schools for the arts and focused on computer literacy for the children.

On the matter of criminal justice, Esquivel pledged nothing new and was proud of his government's record on crime. The PUP leader referred to the 3,714 violent crimes in 1997 and pointed out that while the UDP wasted just under a million on Special Prosecutors, the focus should be on improving the backlog in the Magistrate's Court.

Departing from his party's well known position of no reform, all Esquivel could offer was more excuses. Having already committed the PUP to political reform, Musa committed the party to continue with the consultation process as a partner with civil society.

Mr Esquivel was desperately grabbing at straws as the programme neared the end. He accused PUP candidate Dickie Bradley of inciting violence against the Chinese and Ministers. He attacked the indigenous people in the south for supporting the PUP and hit rock bottom when he insulted the jury system.

Throughout the debate Esquivel distorted irrefutable facts, repeatedly dodged critical questions and conveyed arrogance only displayed by UDP politicians. For Esquivel, the debate was an irritation, unnecessary and uncalled for. Esquivel, like the UDP, doesn't believe he is answerable to the people. Esquivel, like the UDP, doesn't believe he is accountable for his management of the nation. Esquivel, like the UDP, wants Belize to avoid a debate on the UDP record. But the '98 national elections is about the cruel years of '93 to '98."

Election-time political reporting, *Belize Times*, Belize City, July 30, 1998

Modern Elections

The PUP has won all but two of Belize's national general elections. On neither of its two terms in office following election victories in 1984 and 1993, has the UDP been able to secure a consecutive term. As was widely predicted, the PUP won a landslide victory in the August 1998 election, taking 26 out of the 29 seats and 60 percent of the popular vote. The ruling Prime Minister, Manuel Esquivel, lost his seat, while Deputy Prime Minister Dean Barrow only narrowly won his race against Dickie Bradley, who has since been appointed to the Senate. Barrow now leads the three UDP members who retained seats in the new parliament, while George Price, the elder statesman of Belizean politics, was again returned by his constituents in the Pickstock Division of Belize City. In the leadership stakes, however, he has made way for the "Class of '68," with Said Musa becoming Belize's third ever Prime Minister. Assad Shoman became Belize's High Commissioner to the UK, while Evan Hyde's son, Cordel, became the Minister of Education and Sport in the new government.

Political Reform

An increasing number of Belizeans believe that the parliamentary two-party system they inherited from the British is unsuitable and in need of change. Faults critics find in the system include the concentration and centralization of power, the lack of mechanisms for bringing in non-political personnel and expertise, and inadequate checks and balances.

Both the civil society movement, led by the Society for the Promotion of Education and Research (SPEAR), and the PUP have put forward political reform proposals. While civil society campaigners have welcomed the PUP reforms as a step in the right direction, they have been met with a deal of cynicism by some campaigners who believe they do not go far enough and still seek to protect the almost total power of the governing party.

The PUP has proposed replacing the Governor-General with a President as head of state. The President would be elected by a two-thirds majority of the House of Assembly. Elected representatives and senators would sit together in a unicameral assembly, with senators allowed to take part in debates but not to vote. Elected members wishing to change party allegiance would have to resign and submit to a by-election. The cabinet would be limited to two-thirds the elected members of the majority party. There would also be an independent judicial and legal services commission, a separate budget for the administration of the judiciary, a bipartisan elections and boundaries commission and measures to give more autonomy to local government bodies.

Because of the ideological similarity between the two major parties and their concentration on individual attacks, much of the practical debate about Belize's development is carried on outside the realms of party politics. The Belizean civil society which guides and informs this process includes the development and environmental non-governmental organizations (NGOs), the business community represented by the Chamber of Commerce and the Better Business Bureau, the trade union movement and the churches.

Among the NGO community, SPEAR has established itself as an effective campaigning body in support of social progress and human rights, constructively challenging accepted political thinking. Both the revitalized Chamber and recently launched Better Business Bureau are actively and professionally promoting policies that will encourage more productive economic investment in Belize. While not completely able to escape the personality driven conflicts which often hinder the effectiveness of politics in Belize, these and similar organizations are making a positive contribution to the political process.

A Nation in the Making

One generation on from independence, Belize is still a new nation and struggling to find and then stand on its feet in a fast changing political and economic environment. Price's vision of greater integration with Central America and U.S. capital investments providing the backbone to the economy appears to be gradually becoming a reality.

But at the same time Belize needs the relationship with Britain as much as ever, now that other countries within the European Union, most notably Germany, argue for an end to the preferential markets on which Belize's distorted economy relies so heavily. Britain has so far stood firm within the EU in support of Belize and its other former colonial territories.

This is a time of great political and economic change for Belize, as both the U.S. and UK signal the end to their significant involvement, with troop withdrawals and cutbacks in aid programs. Belize is felt to be close to being able to go it alone and while this strikes fear into the hearts of some of the more conservative politicians and business leaders in Belize, it signals the beginning of new relationships and new opportunities.

3   THE ECONOMY: MERCHANT BELIZE

Belize's economy has historically been based on trade, both legal and illegal. The Mayas traded over a wide region; the pirates looted Spanish ships off the Belize coast; the Baymen exported timber; rum and whisky were smuggled into the U.S. during Prohibition, while fuel and other items found their way illegally to German U-boats during the Second World War.

The economy continues to be structured around trade, with the major exports now being sugar, citrus (oranges and grapefruit), bananas, marine products (shrimp and lobster) and garments. Belize is also a transshipment route for Colombian cocaine and is involved to a lesser degree in the production and export of marijuana. The foreign exchange earned from legal exports is only enough to pay for two-thirds of the costs of the major imports—machinery, fuel, food and manufactured goods.

Belize's trade is dominated by its relationships with the European Union and the U.S., and by a narrow range of products; the sugar, banana and citrus industries combined accounted for about 70 percent of export earnings in the first nine months of 1997. Not only does Belize run a high and persistent trade deficit with the rest of the world, but it is also vulnerable to changing world prices for its narrow range of exports, and is reliant on preferential markets for its principal exports of sugar, citrus and bananas.

Belize's trading relationships continue to reflect its status as a former British colony, although this is also changing as Belize becomes more a part of Central America. Belize was one of the founding members of the Caribbean Common Market and Community (Caricom), formed in 1973 by the countries of the English-speaking Caribbean. It is also a member of the British Commonwealth, and the African, Pacific and Caribbean (ACP) countries which have special trade and aid agreements with the European Union under the Lomé Convention. Belize enjoys preferential markets under Lomé for traditional products such as rum, sugar and bananas.

But this system of preferences has been brought into question in the 1990s, especially after legal action by the U.S. government against what it sees as illegal obstacles to free trade. The fourth Lomé Convention expires in 2000, and there are fears that the days of guaranteed entry into Europe for certain commodities and fixed prices for others may one day be terminated. As a result, Belize's government has been promoting diversification of the economy. Sectors being developed include tourism, offshore business and free-zone export facilities, and non-traditional crops such as papayas, cucumber and ginger.

No More Free Money

Gross Domestic Product (GDP) growth of about five percent a year in the 1970s was followed in the 1980s by a period of slow growth, about one percent annually, caused by the collapse of sugar prices. The 1990s were also difficult for the Belizean economy. The withdrawal of the British army garrison in 1993 is estimated to have cost Belize $15 million a year. There have also been sweeping cutbacks in foreign grant aid: U.S. aid to Belize decreased from $12 million to $3 million between 1990 and 1994 and has since dropped even further. Despite this, an export boom and increased tourist revenue enabled Belize to register average annual GDP growth in the 1990s of four percent, while keeping inflation down to a yearly average of three percent. This low inflation can partly be attributed to the Belizean dollar's being pegged at a fixed rate of two to the U.S. dollar.

At the same time, and encouraged by the International Monetary Fund, the government has been forced to embark on a program of structural adjustment to reduce a fiscal imbalance that in 1994 saw government expenditure exceed revenues by $35 million. In 1995 it introduced a public-sector wage freeze and cut over 800 government jobs. It followed this with the introduction in April 1996 of value-added tax (VAT).

Despite their massive unpopularity, these measures had reduced the fiscal imbalance to $6 million by 1997, although by 1998 the deficit was once again on the increase. On the other hand, the budget cuts pushed a high unemployment rate even higher, to 13.8 percent in 1996, but falling slightly to 12.7 percent in 1997.

Employment creation is a major problem facing the economy. With over 39 percent of the population under fourteen, more jobs need to be found. The alternative will be large-scale youth unemployment, with the negative social consequences this is likely to entail. Most Belizeans who do have jobs are employed in the agricultural sector; a 1994 government survey estimated that 22.5 percent of the population was employed in agriculture, 15.4 percent in wholesale and retail trade, 9.7 percent in manufacturing, 9.2 percent in education and health, 7.8 percent in public administration and 6.6 percent in construction.

The Local Market

Belize has a limited local manufacturing sector due to the small local market and its inability to compete on costs of production with its neighbors. Import controls protect what local industry there is, although these are gradually being brought down as Belize introduces the Caribbean Community (Caricom) common external tariff, designed to prevent regional protectionism and encourage free trade. Most manufacturing in Belize is aimed at import-substitution for the local market. Goods produced for domestic consumption include cigarettes, beer, soft drinks and snacks, as well as flour (Belize Mills was recently taken over by the major U.S. multinational, Archer Daniels Midland), fertilizer and batteries.

Belize is largely self-sufficient in rice, beans and maize, although production is very variable and government controls have been necessary to protect producers from cheaper Mexican and Guatemalan imports. Mennonite farmers produce poultry and dairy products on a commercial scale, while production of pork and beef is on a smaller scale, with over 60 percent of pork being produced by small-scale milpa farmers.

Sugar: The Cane Gang

The sugar industry is based in the north of Belize, where some 5,000 farmers cultivate 65,000 acres – half of Belize's arable land acreage – of sugar cane on small, family-run farms. During harvesting, thousands more are employed as seasonal workers. Annual production is about 92,000 metric tons. The farmers belong to the Cane Farmers Association, which organizes quotas and deliveries. Overall co-ordination of the industry is the responsibility of the Belize Sugar Cane Board.

The industry only became important for Belize in the 1960s when the British sugar multinational Tate and Lyle began operating Belize's two sugar processing plants, Libertad and Tower Hill. The production of sugar, as well as its by-product, molasses, became established as Belize's principal economic activity, taking over from the declining timber industry.

A boom in the 1970s, when world sugar prices were high, was followed by a slump in the 1980s, leading to Tate and Lyle's decision to close the Libertad processing plant and divest 90 percent of Tower Hill. Prices picked up, however, and with government help the industry was able to restructure and survive. The Libertad plant was leased out to Petrojam, the Jamaican state oil company, but closed again in 1997. The Tower Hill plant is owned and operated by Belize Sugar Industries, a local company managed by Booker Tate, which has a marketing agreement with Tate and Lyle.

With production back up to peak levels, the industry still faces a number of challenges, as it remains vulnerable to changes in world sugar prices, and heavily dependent on preferential export arrangements with the U.S., Canada and Europe. The U.S. bought almost 17,000 metric tons at above world market prices in 1998-9, while the EU accounted for approximately 40,000 metric tons a year in the 1990s. Without these special export arrangements, Belize, as a high-cost producer, would find it very difficult to compete in open world markets. Belize is in a precarious position, as several other producers such as Mexico or Guatemala, both able to produce sugar far cheaper than Belize, are poised to batter the Belizean industry if

Tugs wait to tow barges out to UK-bound
freighters, Belize City sugar mill   *James Beveridge*

the preferential export agreements ever come to an end. This unenviable position has caused many Belizean cane farmers to begin taking the economic medicine of diversification into other non-traditional crops and activities.

Citrus

The industry was first developed in the 1930s, but sustained development was difficult, given fluctuations in world prices. In the early 1980s, frost and disease in the Florida citrus industry led to a boom in prices, and citrus concentrate became Belize's second biggest revenue earner. The U.S. Caribbean Basin Initiative (CBI) also abolished the 30 percent tariff on concentrate exports to the U.S., further assisting the industry. From the mid-1980s to the mid-1990s production more than tripled and citrus was established as the second most valuable export commodity. Belize is now the third largest supplier of frozen orange and grapefruit concentrate to the U.S. after Mexico and Brazil.

Citrus is exported in two forms – as frozen concentrate, and as a single strength juice. There are some 400 citrus farms that together total 35,000 acres, with the majority in the Stann Creek Valley, and about ten percent of the total acreage in the Cayo District. Most farms are privately owned, and growers belong to the Citrus Growers' Association, a co-operative organization that negotiates with government, purchasers and suppliers on behalf of its members. Many workers in the industry, especially on the larger farms, are Central American immigrants.

The heart of the industry lies a few miles outside Dangriga Town, where two modern citrus processing plants, Belize Food Products (BFP) and the Citrus Company of Belize (CCB), are based. BFP was a subsidiary of Nestlé, which sold out to a local consortium in 1990, and CCB is 51 percent owned by the Trinidad Citrus Association, with the minority shareholding owned by Belizean Growers.

As with sugar, the citrus industry is vulnerable, despite record production levels and the recent expansion into production of single-strength juice. Despite increased production in 1997, the fall in world prices still caused earnings from citrus exports to fall.

Bananas: Profits out of Poverty

Belize's banana industry is dominated by a handful of wealthy individuals and the Irish multinational, Fyffes. Fourteen individuals own the country's fourteen farms, and Fyffes has a shareholding in one farm and markets all Belize's bananas in Europe. Whereas in other parts of the Caribbean, most notably the Windward Islands, there is a social dimension to banana cultivation, with much production in the hands of independent small farmers, in Belize the situation is different. The industry is highly profitable, and the rewards of the industry are shared between individual farm owners and Fyffes. The benefit to the local economy is limited and the industry employs mainly low-wage non-unionized immigrant labor. As bananas are harvested and shipped every week, bringing much-needed foreign exchange into the economy, the industry holds a strong bargaining card with government and plays it to full advantage.

The banana business in Belize did have a more socially equitable beginning when, at the turn of the century, many small growers received small parcels of land in the Stann Creek Valley. The initial success of the industry attracted the attentions of the U.S. multinational, the United Fruit Company, which bought up many of the small farms. But the industry was subsequently plagued by Panama disease and other problems, and without the necessary support, banana production plummeted in the 1930s and the industry eventually failed.

Fyffes Times Better?

Initial efforts to revitalize Belize's banana industry in the 1970s and 1980s were beset by poor management and lack of investment. Despite having access to the preferential market in the UK that gave market support to former and existing colonies, the industry ran up large debts with the government and the banks. Faced with the possibility of closure, the

Citrus orchards   *James Beveridge*

government, the banks, the banana industry and Fyffes, which all had a vested interest in maintaining production, worked out an emergency rescue package. The industry was restructured in the early 1990s with the Banana Growers' Association (BGA), the growers' co-operative, taking over control of the running of the industry and a number of farms that had been in the public sector.

Belize has since developed its banana industry into the country's third most important foreign exchange earner, although the industry has come under severe international criticism for alleged abuses of its workers, including the stifling of attempts by its workers to form a trade union.

The industry increased production during the 1990s in the hope that the EU would increase its 55,000 metric ton quota. The EU did not agree to the increase, so in 1996 Belize had to dump the equivalent of 100,000 boxes of bananas that had been produced in excess of the quota. In 1997 a number of the farms in the industry shut down while others had to cut back on their acreage. By 1998, the industry was left with only fourteen privately owned farms harvesting 3,600 acres. The late 1990s have been filled with uncertainty following the World Trade Organization (WTO) ruling against the EU in a case brought by the U.S. and four Latin American countries against its banana marketing regime. The EU has announced changes to the regime, including the replacement of country quotas by an overall quota of 857,700 metric tons for all ACP producers, and abolition of the present licensing system. Belizean banana producers stand to benefit from the removal of the national quota ceiling, but the U.S. and its allies have indicated that they may renew their WTO challenge to the EU despite the changes.

Sea Food: Co-operative Success

The marine products industry has grown in importance since the early 1960s and is now a major source of foreign exchange and a vital source of food for the local market. There are thirteen fishing co-operatives in Belize, of which the four largest – Caribeña, the Northern, the National and Placencia – dominate the export industry. These four organizations provide credit, marketing and distribution facilities for their 800 members. In addition to the co-operatives, there are also an estimated 400 independent fisherman.

The major problems the industry faces are over-fishing and out-of-season poaching, mainly of products such as lobster and conch. The government needs to be able to enforce its adequate fishing regulations to ensure that supplies are not permanently depleted.

Lobsters, along with shrimp, are also produced by Belize's rapidly expanding fish farming industry. Recent investment of over $18 million is likely to see this sector soon overtake the banana industry as the third biggest export earner in Belize. There are currently six shrimp farms in operation, the majority of which are foreign owned. The two largest farms, Nova and Laguna Madre, also operate processing and packaging plants. Nova recently assumed responsibility for the management of Laguna Madre and its sister farm, Cherax.

Export Manufacturing

Belize's small export production includes garment production and some agricultural processing. The "offshore" garment industry is the only example of large-scale export manufacturing in Belize. The industry, which is based at the Williamson Industries factory in Ladyville, north of Belize City, is foreign-owned and makes imported clothing for re-export to the U.S. under the "Dickies" label.

Despite employing non-unionized labor and operating in a tax-free environment, Belize's garment industry finds it difficult to compete on cost. Between 1993 and 1997 production fell by half, from 4.3 million to 2 million units, mainly as a result of increased competition from Mexico. The drop in export earnings over the same period, however, from $20.3 million to $17.8 million, was not so severe.

Agricultural processing for export is concentrated on the production of molasses, though there has been a sharp fall in this activity following the 1997 closure of the Libertad molasses factory.

Mining, Energy, Construction and Utilities

Of the several mineral products known to exist in Belize, only dolomite limestone is produced in anything like commercial quantities. A dolomite fertilizer plant opened in 1992 with a production potential of 80,000 tons per year. Gold, bauxite, barytes, cassiterite and gypsum are also found but either are not available in commercial quantities or are not exploited commercially.

Belize's oil needs of approximately 600,000 barrels per year are supplied by a monthly tanker from the U.S. company, Exxon. In 1988, Belize signed the San José Accord with Mexico under which it is able to receive crude oil on a concessionary basis. In the mid-1990s a supplementary agreement was signed, allowing Belize to receive up to 1,000 barrels a day of refined oil on the same basis.

Several companies have drilled exploratory oil wells in Belize, most recently in January 1996 when a consortium of four companies was granted a license to drill a $6 million offshore exploratory well southwest of Glover's Reef. As yet no commercial oil deposits have been found.

Construction is a major employer, but most large-scale construction is dependent on capital funds from international donor agencies and is relatively short-term. The Belize City Infrastructure Project, the Karl Heusner Memorial Hospital, the Central Bank, the upgrading of the International Airport, and the Hummingbird and Southern Highways have been the major capital projects undertaken during the 1990s. These have provided employment and injected significant resources into the local economy, though much of the finance is in the form of long-term loans, which have increased Belize's national debt.

The government began a program of privatization in the late 1980s and early 1990s. Belize Telecommunications Limited (BTL) was sold between 1988 and 1992, with 25 percent of its shares now owned by the U.S. telecommunications giant, MCI Communications, 25 percent by the UK-owned multinational holding company, Belize Holdings International (BHI), 27 percent by the Belize Social Security Board, 20 percent by members of the public and the remainder by the Belize government. Despite only having a subscriber base of 29,000 customers, BTL is highly profitable, and has invested in the latest communications technology including a modern fiber optic network and internet services.

The public-run Belize Electricity Board was closed in 1993, and replaced by Belize Electricity Limited (BEL), in which government retained a 61 percent holding. The remainder was sold to the public, with BHI purchasing a 20 percent stake. Most of BEL's electricity has historically been supplied by diesel-powered generators located in each of the major towns. Now BEL is close to completing a national electricity network, and will be able to supply electricity purchased from Mexico and generated at a new 25-mw hydroelectric power station in Mollejon in western Belize. The hydro, completed in 1995 by two U.S. companies under a private joint venture, has been plagued by controversy and setbacks, including construction defects that saw parts of the hydro structure washed away during the first heavy rains. There have also been arguments over the fairness of the terms of the agreement under which electricity is sold to BEL.

Finance and Aid

There are three foreign commercial banks in Belize: Atlantic Bank (Honduras), Barclays (UK) and the Bank of Nova Scotia. In 1987 the Belizean assets of the Royal Bank of Canada were sold to Belize Bank, which is owned by BHI. The commercial banks have been criticized for their conservative lending policy and their high rates of interest. The discount rate has been set at twelve percent since 1989, and the typical lending rate is about sixteen percent and the deposit rate about eight percent. There are restrictions on the purchase of U.S. dollars, with Central Bank authorization needed for some transactions.

Credit unions are an important source of personal credit, and there are 23 such organizations with an estimated membership of 43,000 and total assets of $52 million. Most credit union loans fund major household purchases or housing construction, as opposed to productive projects.

The government-run Development Finance Corporation (DFC), founded in 1963, is the primary source of development aid finance. This channels mainly international aid money into development projects, concentrating in the agricultural and construction sectors. Interest rates charged by DFC tend to be lower than those charged by the commercial banks, and the projects financed are usually higher risk.

Belize is still heavily dependent on this kind of foreign aid, especially for capital projects; between 1989 and 1994 Belize received on average $16.2 million per year in aid. The figure remains high today, although more aid is now given in the form of long-term loans as opposed to grants, and the sources of aid are changing.

Traditionally bilateral aid from the U.S., UK, and Canada has been the most significant, but aid now comes increasingly from multilateral organizations such as the Caribbean Development Bank, the Inter-American Development Bank (which Belize joined in 1992), the World Bank and the EU. A high percentage of aid for social programs in Belize is now channeled through the Social Investment Fund, a government body set up under the aegis of the World Bank to offset the negative social effects of structural adjustment.

Belize has also successfully diversified its aid base with loans from the Kuwaiti government (following Belize's support of Kuwait during the Gulf War) and the Taiwanese government. In 1996 Belize consolidated a number of outstanding debts into a new $26 million loan from Taiwan's Export-Import Bank. Belize's debt position was further helped by Britain's announcement that it would convert part of its long-term British aid debt into grants for social projects.

Diversifying the Economy

Diversification has been a common theme in economic policy in Belize since the beginning of the twentieth century, when the colonial government attempted to diversify the forestry-based economy. The current threat to preferential markets established under these earlier diversification programs has refocused government attention on the need to develop new alternatives.

The main focus of this diversification effort has been on shifting away from traditional export crops and toward developing the service economy, most notably tourism, and financial and offshore services. There have also been steps taken to promote the production of non-traditional crops, to increase value-added agricultural processing, and to encourage manufacturing business to relocate to Belize with Export Processing Zones and other tax incentives.

Tourism

The tourism industry in Belize has developed into a major income earner. Attracted by Belize's reputation for unspoiled natural resources, and its English-speaking people, annual tourist arrivals have risen from 60,000 in the 1980s, to over 134,000 in 1997, earning Belize almost $90 million. The premier attractions are the reef and the cayes, with many tourists spending little or no time on mainland Belize. Other attractions are the forests and the Maya ruins. In 1996 Belize ratified the Mundo Maya agreement with Guatemala, Mexico, Honduras and El Salvador under which the five countries co-operate to promote tourism connected with their Maya archeological sites.

One of Belize's first tourists was the Anglo-Portuguese Baron Henry Bliss who visited Belize in 1926 aboard his yacht, the *Sea King*. He enjoyed himself to the extent that he left almost $2 million to Belize. Interest earned on this legacy has helped fund clinics, libraries, water systems, and museums. Modern-day tourists are also a source of income, but there are concerns about the legacy they will leave.

Until the first United Democratic Party (UDP) government was elected in 1984, the previous PUP administrations had done little to encourage tourism. This was partly because of their ideological distaste for service-based industry. Tourism was left to develop on a small scale under the guidance of avid nature and diving enthusiasts. This established the course of the industry as "high-quality, low-quantity" tourism for adventurous travelers interested in nature, especially diving. Most Belize's resorts are correspondingly small-scale (the 360 hotels in Belize have only 3,690 rooms), and specialize in eco- and adventure-tourism. While this approach has meant Belize has avoided the worst excesses of large-scale package tourism, a number of common problems associated with tourism are beginning to surface.

Eco-Tourism: Coca-Cola and the Programme for Belize

Among Belize's several eco-tourism destinations, the one that stands out as a model of environment-friendly business is the Programme for Belize's (PFB) tourism operation on its 228,000-acre Rio Bravo Conservation and Management Area (RBCMA).

The RBMCA was originally part of the giant BEC estate that local businessman Barry Bowen purchased in the 1980s. He sold a large tract to Coca-Cola, who wanted to plant citrus as a guarantee against crop failures in the U.S. Coca-Cola helped create the Programme for Belize in 1989 when it donated 42,000 acres of land representing three major habitats – forest, savannah and marsh – in response to the Massachusetts Audubon Society's appeal for the creation of a bird sanctuary in northern Belize.

Pressure from environmental groups eventually forced Coca-Cola to abandon its plans for citrus production and it passed its remaining 50,000 acres to the PFB in 1992. The remaining 136,000 acres were purchased by the PFB through a fundraising drive in Europe and North America.

With over 240 species of trees, 390 species of birds and 70 known species of mammals, the RBMCA represents one of Belize's highest concentrations of biodiversity.

To generate income for its forest management program, the PFB has entered the tourism industry and offers on-site accommodation, including modern conservation technology, for tourists interested in conservation and research. Areas in which research is currently being carried out include selective logging, chicle production, and micro-propagation (laboratory production of orchids and tropical houseplants for export). The PFB is also working with the communities

Catching a barracuda   *James Beveridge*

in the area to promote economically and environmentally viable activities, including the production of handicrafts for sale to visitors.

Over 1,000 students visit the RBCMA every year, and the PFB hosts "Save the Rainforest" courses, which provide terrestrial and marine ecology education for both Belizean and international students. This combination of research, conservation and education, alongside income-generation and the development of economic opportunities with local people, is beginning to yield results. While in 1997 the PFB estimated the RBCMA to be only 51 percent self-sustaining, that figure is set to increase as new tourist facilities and new economic activities come online.

Problems and Policy

The industry has undoubtedly had some negative consequences, especially for residents of the most popular destinations, Ambergris Caye/ San Pedro, Caye Caulker and Placencia. Land prices have escalated, driven up by land speculators and resort developers. The industry is dominated by foreigners, mainly Americans, Canadians and British, and an increasing number of holiday packages are being sold through travel agencies located outside Belize. While Belize may not have the all-inclusive resorts associated with the package holiday market, it does face the same problems of tourist dollars not hitting the local economy and the foreign domination of the industry.

Another major concern is the impact of tourism on the environment, particularly the coral reef. This is being closely monitored, but there is undoubtedly damage being done despite the government and industry's best efforts. There are also costs associated with upgrading infrastructural facilities; for example, San Pedro needed new sewage facilities to cope with the number of tourists visiting the island. Belize's Philip Goldson

International Airport has also needed improvements, in order to cope with increased tourist arrivals.

While there are issues to be faced, the industry in Belize is marked by an acute awareness of its market. Both the government and the industry play an active role in developing tourism policy, and in 1998 combined to produce the first National Tourism Plan. The issues dealt with in the plan include encouraging more locally-run tourism facilities, training and certification of people involved in the industry, quality control, managing growth and developing connections between tourism and other sectors of the economy.

Non-Traditional Crops and Agricultural Processing

The promotion of alternatives to the big three traditional export crops has had mixed results. Cocoa production was once thought to offer great potential, but a project funded by the government, USAID, and Hershey (the U.S. chocolate multinational) failed to meet projected output. Hershey eventually pulled out of Belize; production by 1993 had fallen to only 158,600 pounds compared to the forecast 10,000 metric tons. A UK company, Green and Black, revived hopes of a recovery in 1994, contracting to pay farmers in the San José area £0.48/lb until November 1997. The export of fresh vegetables to the U.S., started under the CBI, has also failed to meet expectations.

Attention has recently switched to tropical fruits such as mango and papaya. USAID helped fund the Orange Walk-based Belize Agri-Business Company (BABCO) which concentrates on the production and marketing of papaya for export. Some of the major banana and citrus farmers in the south are also investing heavily in the production of both papaya and mango. While neither fruit has yet become a significant export, the signs are that this will be achieved over the next few years. There has also been some success with the export of habanero peppers to the U.S. market. A Belmopan-based company, Food Limited, is the major purchaser and exporter of peppers, which are produced mainly by small farmers in surrounding immigrant communities.

Rice is believed by some experts to offer great potential. Belize is already self-sufficient in rice (and bean) production, and with suitable investment this could become a viable export industry. Another option is livestock production, which is concentrated in the north of Belize. Inroads have been made into the Caribbean meat market with exports of beef to Jamaica, but the industry needs more modern slaughter and processing facilities if it is to become a significant export earner.

The uncertainties surrounding primary agriculture have led to much greater attention being paid to the need for the processing of agricultural commodities. There is also a great deal of waste resulting from the strict quality requirements of the export industry (8,000 metric tons of bananas a year are dumped because they fail to meet quality guidelines). The success of the two citrus processing plants has shown that Belize is capable of managing the latest processing technology, but the expansion of processing facilities is hindered by the size of investment required, uncertain markets and doubts over the reliability of agricultural production.

The agro-processing industry is in its early stages, but markets have already been established for a range of dehydrated products such as pepper and mango. Several of the larger banana and citrus farmers in the South of the country are investing in dehydration technology to exploit the existing markets, and are developing new ones.

Offshore Services and the Financial Sector

Belize, emulating several other Caribbean territories, is developing a range of offshore services. These include company and ship registrations, and offshore banking and financial services. This sector is still in its infancy, although there is clearly great potential. The growth of the offshore sector is limited by the lack of technical expertise within Belize, lack of necessary legal and financial structures, and some nervousness about the degree to which such activities might compromise Belize's economic independence.

A specialized offshore service that was until recently being seriously considered was the hosting of internet gambling. Belize has a sophisticated telecommunications system, bearing in mind its small subscriber base, and this attracted gambling entrepreneurs from certain U.S. states where gambling is illegal. But disagreements between the government and the investors put a halt to the development of this venture.

While organizations like the Chamber of Commerce and the Better Business Bureau are actively seeking investment in Belize, investment growth is limited by the lack of a developed financial sector and by concerns over the security of investments. In the early 1990s the government passed "International Business Company" (IBC) legislation to encourage international companies to come to Belize by allowing them to operate in a tax-free environment. Options now being considered include the development of a capital market and the strengthening of legal protection for investors.

A Family Affair

Business and politics in Belize are a family affair, awash with colorful characters. A few rich and powerful families control the vast majority of business and their undisputed king is nomadic businessman Michael Ashcroft. Ashcroft, head of Belize Holdings and now a major player in the financial affairs of the British Conservative Party, has at some point had a hand in most of Belize's major businesses, although now his interests spread far and wide, into the Caribbean, the U.S., and Europe. His future involvement in Belize, however, is in some doubt.

Wealthy Businessman Leaving Belize?

"Michael Ashcroft, one of Belize's wealthiest residents and a naturalized citizen, has said he plans to leave Belize and set up new camp in the Turks and Caicos Islands, according to a report in *The Wall Street Journal*, taking with him the headquarters of his BHI Corp., which owns Belize Bank, a 90% stake in the Radisson Fort George Hotel, a one-half stake in Belize Food Holdings, a one-quarter stake in Belize Telecommunications, and a one-fifth stake in Belize Electricity. Ashcroft, 50 years old, English by birth, and occasionally controversial in Britain, the U.S., and in Belize, controls 65% of BHI, which is traded on the NASDAQ exchange in the U.S. The businessman reportedly considers the current UDP government as less than completely friendly to his company's interests, as in 1995 it proposed repealing part of a 1990 act that gave BHI and some other corporations sizeable tax breaks. Although spokespersons for BHI declined to comment on the possible move to the Turks and Caicos, a small island group near Haiti that was hard hit by hurricanes earlier this year, BHI financial reports do indicate that the company is focusing on expansion outside of Belize."

Report from *Belize First* Magazine

"BHI also announced that it has agreed to sell all of its discontinued operations for $15.6m, which represents net asset value, to an investor group led by Allan Forrest who has been managing BHI's non-financial businesses in Central America. Businesses that are included in the sale are Johnston International Limited, Hadsphaltic International Limited, Leeward Limited, Bearwood Corporate Services Limited, Belize Aggregates Limited and Belize Leisure Limited (owner of the Radisson Fort George Hotel in Belize City). Other discontinued assets being sold include Belize Food Holdings Limited (26.7%), Great Belize Productions Limited (36.2%) and Energia Global International, Ltd. (19.5%)."

Belize Holdings Press Release, September 1998

Other Belizean businessmen such as Barry Bowen, the Feinstein, Zabaneh and Habet families, Santiago Castillo, and the expatriate Jamaicans, Pat Polack and Mike Duncker, while not having Ashcroft's international savvy, have all made fortunes in Belize. Bowen's empire is based on his bottling business, which sells Coca Cola and the local Belikin beer throughout the country. No Mayan village is complete without a couple of bars selling Barry Bowen's drinks.

The others vie for their share of the lucrative hardware market supplying Belize's housing and capital projects boom, as well as for their share of the profits from Belize's protected agricultural markets. Of the international money that poured into Belize in the last decade, that which was not exported straight back out again landed in the pockets of one of the fortunate few. The close relationship between Belize's business and political community, while not implying any wrongdoing, seems to provide evidence that to get ahead in Belize means following the old Creole sayings of "hand wash hand" or, more appropriately, "one hand can't clap."

Newer members of the family include Soeren Soerenson, whose burgeoning Belize business empire is linked to the Danish aid organization, Humana International, once the subject of a European Commission inquiry into the overlap between its charitable and commercial work.

Free Market Fears

As we have seen, the Belizean economy is very reliant on external support. Aid grants and loans fund most of the capital expenditure and social programs, while preferential markets support the exports needed to pay for Belize's high consumption of imports. The prospect of "free trade" fills Belizeans with dread, as the country is surrounded by low-cost high-volume producers with whom Belize, with its limited infrastructure, higher nominal wages and small local market, cannot possibly compete.

At the same time, many of Belize's best educated young people leave in search of better prospects in the U.S., Canada or Europe, replaced by poorly educated farmers from neighboring republics attracted by the availability of land and work in the citrus and banana industries. Social services are over-stretched by a population growing at four percent a year, and the IMF-prescribed structural adjustment program is placing restraints on the government's room to maneuver. The threat of devaluation, which would reduce already low real wages and drive up inflation, is ever present as Belize struggles to find the foreign currency it needs to pay its import bill.

The situation, however, is not entirely gloomy. The population growth may soon begin to benefit the economy, as the local market expands to a size where it can sustain more local industry; new locally produced goods such as snacks and drinks are already beginning to appear. The immigration of the 1980s, as well as providing labor for the citrus and banana industry, has also increased small-scale agricultural production, mainly of vegetables. The full import-substitution effects of this are yet to be felt.

Given limited agricultural land, the government has to make a choice between more plantation agriculture for export or smaller-scale agriculture for domestic consumption. Ultimately, the end of preferential markets may force this choice in favor of food for local markets. The negative impact of plantation agriculture includes soils being permanently damaged by intensive farming, and the social impact of the 5,000 immigrant workers now settled around the southern citrus and banana plantations.

The treatment of these immigrants has been the cause of repeated concern from human rights organizations. Complaints include low contract-based pay, poor housing facilities, intimidation of those attempting to form trade unions, sexual abuse of women workers, withholding of passports and other papers, and indiscriminate hiring and firing. Immigrant women are especially vulnerable, and sexual abuse appears to be widespread both within the home and within the working environment. There is also a small but growing sex industry in Belize that employs mainly young immigrant women.

The other group most often at the base of the economic ladder are the Mayans. Plantation agriculture has impinged on Mayan farming practices. Some Mayans are being forced into work in plantation agriculture to pay for the purchase of imported foodstuffs which they could, but for lack of land, easily produce themselves. This distortion of the local economy, and the inequitable power relationship resulting from the distortion, is a strong argument against the continuation of export-oriented plantation agriculture in Belize.

The most important challenge facing the economy is how to tackle the macro-economic situation while giving the most vulnerable groups in Belize's society hope and dignity. The challenge facing Belize's government and civil society, especially the private sector, human rights organizations, and trade unions, is to work together to build an economy that is equitable as well as sustainable.

4   PEOPLE AND CULTURE: "A MOTLEY CREW"

"For one thing, Belize was not an island, and Britain could not apply, as it did on other (Caribbean) islands, the concept that it was dealing with an empty land and that it could build a society 'from scratch.' The indigenous people of the islands were effectively eliminated (and when they were not, as in the case of the Garifuna, they were simply deported), but the Maya were not.

They were here, and they kept on coming, and the British were forced to deal with this reality. And more people kept on coming, and it was this motley crew, as they procreated, mixed with one another and continued to live here, that gradually carried out the process of creating the nation state of Belize."

This passage by Assad Shoman, the Belizean activist and writer, sums up the process by which modern Belize came about. It is a multi-layered society and while the old social order, headed by the mockingly named "Royal Creoles," still dominates economic and political life, there is undoubtedly a change happening as Belize adapts to the reality of its population.

While Creole culture still dominates, Belize's Creole population is becoming relatively less influential due to continuing Hispanic immigration and Creole emigration to the U.S., Canada and Europe. The ethnic makeup of the population shows that the largest single ethnic group is *mestizo* (of mixed Spanish and Maya origin), accounting for about 44 percent of the population.

A Diverse Nation

Belize's diversity is reflected in the number of different ethnic groups – Creole, mestizo, Maya, Garifuna, Chinese, East Indian, Arab, and European. Within each main ethnic group are further subdivisions based on geography, culture and language. The mestizo population, for example, includes descendants of those who fled the Caste War in Mexico's Yucatán, as well as refugees and immigrants from Guatemala, Honduras and El Salvador. Belize contains three distinct Maya communities – Mopan and Ke'kchi Maya in the west and south, and Yucatec Maya in the north. The Mennonites also have several distinctive communities that are usually divided into "modernists" and "traditionalists."

An increasing number of people are at least bi-lingual, with Creole, English and Spanish being the main languages. Garifuna also have their

Creole family in Crooked Tree village   *James Beveridge*

own language, also called Garifuna, derived from the language spoken by the Caribs of St. Vincent, with French and African influences. Each of the three Maya groups speak their own language, which is incomprehensible to the others. Belize's Mennonite community speaks a Low German dialect, and the more recent arrivals among Belize's East Indian community speak Hindi. There is also a growing Taiwanese/Chinese community that introduces even more cultural and linguistic diversity.

Creole Belize—"We Da Fu Ya, Everybody Else Da Come Ya"

The dominant language and culture in Belize is Creole, the mixture of British and African elements that evolved from the interaction of the European settlers and African slaves brought over from Jamaica and elsewhere in the Caribbean. The term "Creole" is often a confusing one as it can have different meanings. It usually refers to three things: language, culture and ethnicity. The Creole language is a derivative of English with some African words and grammar and can, with practice, be understood by English speakers. The children of new immigrants into Belize are taught solely in English, but most end up speaking Creole before, or instead of, English. Creole is the language of the street.

Belizean Creole culture is harder to define, especially with the increase in external cultural influences, from the Caribbean, the U.S. and neighboring Hispanic countries. While some may argue that these influ-

Flora and Fauna of Belize

Jaguar

All photos by Jim Beveridge

Queen
angel
fish and
sponges

Black orchid - Belize's
national flower

Scuba diver and coral

Both inland and offshore, Belize is home to an extraordinary variety of birds, animals, plants and marine life. However, increasingly its natural inhabitants are under threat and the following numbers make sober reading: birds - 533 native species (33 threatened); mammals - 155 native species (15 threatened); reptiles - 107 native species (7 threatened). The coral reef is also increasingly being damaged by the impact of the tourism and agriculture industries so crucial to Belize's economy. So while Belize overflows with natural beauty it is also a fragile beauty which needs to be carefully nurtured and protected.

Cattle-heart butterfly

Black howler monkey

Rufustail hummingbird feeding at costus

Heliconia - a rainforest flower

Red-eyed tree
frog on costus

ences are enriching, Creole culture may be being diluted to the point where it exists as no more than language. In its present-day form, it is the result of centuries of the intermingling of African and European culture. The European settlers in Belize believed their culture to be superior and imposed it on their African slaves. The slaves' expressions of African culture were a symbol of resistance to this European domination and soon a cultural synthesis was taking place, out of which emerged Creole culture.

It is a culture with its roots in a struggle against oppression, and celebration in the face of hardship. Women were especially important in developing this form of cultural expression. While male slaves usually lived in remote mahogany camps and had opportunities to fight back and physically escape slavery, women slaves most often lived in servants' quarters in Belize City and their culture became their only means to retain their dignity and identity. The Creole language was vital as it allowed slaves to communicate among themselves, and along with music and drama it proved critical in keeping alive African traditions and helping the slaves mock the European sense of superiority.

Language is the most evident element of modern Creole culture. Dance, music, and food are also important. Creole cooking includes the staple Belizean diet of rice and beans, Creole bread, and dishes such as cow foot soup and pepperpot, a stew made from any combination of ingredients. While there are traditional Creole music styles such as Brukdown, modern Belizean Creole music and dance is, like pepperpot, a mixed bag, reflecting the wide range of influences and Belize's position at the cultural crossroads between Europe, the Caribbean and Central America, and the U.S., Mexico and South America.

Ethnically, the term Creole in Belize usually describes a Belizean born in Belize descended from the European settlers and/or Africans, but excluding Garifuna who are treated as a separate ethnic group. Creoles account for less than 30 percent of the population. A small group of Creoles, the so-called "Royal Creoles" have traditionally dominated Belize's political and business community. The term "Royal Creole" was coined to indicate the high status of these families within Belize society, a very influential few who are often direct descendants of Belize's wealthier settler class. But by far the majority of Belize's Creole community is poor and black, based in and around Belize City and the Belize River Valley.

As Belize matures and distinctions between the various ethnic groups blur, it will become harder to define a separate Creole class of people. Many Belizeans descended from mestizo and other immigrants would consider themselves to be Creole. A term that is often used to denote this wider group is "Roots Belizean." This phrase was used in the 1993 elections by politicians wanting to stir up feelings against new immigrants. In practice, it is not easy to actually define who is or is not a Roots Belizean. The most obvious contenders to the title are the Maya, though this is not exactly what the politicians had in mind.

The Maya

Whereas a million or more Maya may once have inhabited the area known as Belize, their present-day descendants now number only around 25,000. Archeologists, anthropologists and historians are still struggling to piece together the full story of this people who are Belize's longest continuous inhabitants.

Belize's contemporary Maya population is spread throughout the country. The Yucatec Maya in the north are generally more assimilated into Belizean life than the Mopan and Ke'kchi Maya in the south who live mainly in isolated rural villages. Many Mayan families live traditional lives as subsistence farmers in small communities of palm-thatched houses that have little inside except hammocks and wood-burning stoves. Traditions are changing, however, and it is now not uncommon, even in some of the more remote villages, to see cement-block houses, televisions, pool bars, and grocery stores.

Most families are subsistence milpa farmers, raising their own chickens and pigs, and growing their own beans and corn. The staple food is *masa*, a corn dough used to make tortillas. Large-scale community projects are usually carried out under the communal *fajina* system, in which time is contributed by family members toward works beneficial to the entire community.

The destructive nature of Belize's two-party system is most evident in Maya communities. Elections in Belize often hinge on very few votes and politicians anxiously cultivate support by bestowing privileges via their representatives to potential supporters in each village. Villages are often split in two because of the ill-guided actions of politicians desperate for political power, and whole villages can be victimized for supporting the wrong party.

Another dividing force in Maya communities has been organized religion. While many Maya, under the influence of evangelizing Spanish priests, turned to Catholicism, missionaries from other religions have introduced further divisions. It is not uncommon to find a Maya village split between, for example, Catholic and Baptist, with one group refusing to work with the other on community projects.

The problems of land security and rights are the major concern, especially as traditional Maya communal landholdings are inadequately dealt with in Belizean law. The needs of plantation agriculture and land specu-

Mayan sisters   *Martin Mowforth*

lators seem to have been of greater concern to consecutive governments than Mayan rights. Recent events such as the lack of consultation with the Maya over the paving of the Southern Highway and the granting of logging concessions in the Columbia Forest Reserve, highlight the urgent need to resolve these issues.

Faced with ever increasing contacts with the rest of Belize and by questions over land, the Maya have become better represented through their own organizations and through links with international indigenous rights bodies. Their actions have made the government and others sit up and take notice. The message from these organizations is that the Maya want to be part of Belize, but they want their views and their culture to be respected and to be able to deal with change on their own terms.

Hispanic Influences

It is all too easy to imagine Belize City as an island of Caribbean Creole culture in an Hispanic sea. Surrounded by Hispanic countries with a population of over 100 million, some in Belize have adopted a siege mentality and the more extreme politicians play to this view with talk of "floods" of immigration.

The reality is that Belize is already a Hispanic country, with mestizos accounting for 44 percent of the population. On two occasions, Belize's population has swelled with a large scale Hispanic immigration—during the Caste War in the mid-nineteenth century and the Central American civil wars of the 1980s. Given the continued emigration by Creole Belizeans to the U.S. and immigration of Central Americans seeking land and work, it is likely that the latinization of Belize will continue.

The northern towns of Orange Walk and Corozal already have a strongly Hispanic flavor, since most of the refugees from the Yucatán settled here in the nineteenth century. The western towns of San Ignacio, Santa Elena and Benque Viejo are also all predominantly Hispanic. Around the capital, Belmopan, several large refugee settlements, including Valley of Peace and Armenia, have become permanent communities. In the south, Central Americans, attracted as ostensibly seasonal workers to the citrus and banana industries, have established permanent villages.

The impact of this new influence in Belize can be felt in a number of ways. First, the obvious signs include the Latino music played in clubs and on the radio and the restaurants serving Hispanic foods such as burritos, tacos, and garnaches. Most newspapers now include a Spanish section, and there are several Spanish-speaking radio stations. Even so, it is probably in the economy that the influence is most keenly felt.

The Hispanic population is closely associated with agriculture; in the north the sugar industry took off after the immigration from the Yucatán and it is the descendants of these original immigrants who now run the industry. In the south, the citrus and banana industries rely on Hispanic labor for fieldwork and harvesting. And in the west many recent immigrants now run small-scale farming operations, growing vegetables, watermelons, beans and corn. This agricultural tradition has proved immensely valuable to Belize in generating foreign exchange and substituting locally produced foodstuffs for imports.

There have been some problems associated with the legal assimilation of the more recent immigrants. Many have applied for Belizean residency and nationality, but the lack of government resources, political interference, and the opposition of some Belizean officials in processing these applications have combined to cause a degree of ill feeling. Recent evidence shows that most immigrants receive nationality documents around election time when their votes can be crucial in deciding the election outcome. A study by Belize non-governmental organizations of events surrounding the 1993 elections found widespread political abuse in the issuing of nationality documents to immigrants. The same abuse appeared to have been repeated in the 1998 elections.

The political power of the Hispanic community is being increasingly felt. Florencio Marin, a mestizo politician from the north of the country, won considerable support in his leadership challenge following the resignation of George Price as leader of the PUP in 1996. Both of Belize's two main political parties realize the importance of appealing to the mestizo population and so increasingly appoint mestizo and/or Spanish-speaking candidates, and campaign in both English and Spanish.

Garifuna man grating coconut
for cooking oil

James Beveridge

The Garifuna

A coastal people by tradition, the Garifuna have a pattern of spreading and establishing village communities along the Caribbean coastline, from Dangriga (the capital of the Stann Creek District) in Belize to Pearl Lagoon in Nicaragua. The first reported Garifuna settlement in Belize was in November 1802, and Belize's Garifuna population remains concentrated along the country's southern coast. Most are involved in fishing, farming and public service professions such as teaching, healthcare and the civil service; many of the government employees in the rural villages in the south of Belize are Garifuna.

There is close contact between Belize's Garifunas and other Garifuna communities in Central America, such as Livingstone on the Guatemalan coast. Garifuna culture and history are kept alive through regular national and regional cultural events and conferences, which attempt to promote learning and understanding and to offset the negative cultural effects of the ever-increasing exposure to outside influences.

Belize's Garifuna (or Garinagu) community trace its roots back to the Caribs, who with indigenous Arawak Indians, had emigrated out of South America beginning in 160 AD. They settled the island Caribbean, and at the time of the first European contact in 1492, were based in the Lesser Antilles. Militarily well-organized, the Caribs regularly raided Arawak territories, killing the men and taking the women as wives. A language evolved with a female Arawak version and a male Carib version, which were distinct yet mutually intelligible. This pattern of language survives today in the modern Central American Garifuna language.

While the Arawak population was all but wiped out within fifty years by the colonizing Europeans, the Caribs fought back, and the French finally opted to befriend them. As a result, some French words found their way into the Carib language, French surnames were adopted, and French priests gradually converted the Caribs to Roman Catholicism.

Then, in 1635, a Spanish slave ship carrying West Africans to the Caribbean was wrecked in a storm near Bequia, St. Vincent. A number of African survivors swam ashore and were welcomed by the Caribs. Through inter-marriage the race of "Black Caribs," or Garifuna was born. The Africans quickly adopted Carib language, culture and religion, although keeping the African drum for secular and sacred music as well as the practice of ancestral worship.

In March 1795, the French persuaded Chatoyer, then leader of the Caribs, to mount an attack on the British. With the Caribs close to victory, a British soldier challenged Chatoyer to a sword duel. According to legend, Chatoyer believed no man born of woman could kill him and accepted the challenge, only to be fatally wounded. He died on March 14, 1795. The Caribs continued to fight under the command of Chatoyer's brother, Duvalle, but in June of 1796 they were finally forced to surrender.

The British then began their plans to colonize St. Vincent. In October 1796, 5,080 Caribs were taken by British ships to the island of Balliceaux off the coast of St. Vincent. More than half the population died during the next six months. A fleet of eight ships took the survivors, 2,248 Garifuna, to the island of Roatán off the coast of Honduras. A further 242 people died on this journey and only 2,026 Garifuna arrived in Roatán on April 12, 1797. From there they were to spread throughout Central America.

A Living Culture

Many Garifuna are tri-lingual, speaking English and Spanish along with their own language. Cultural activities such as traditional singing and drumming, and sacred ceremonies such as the *dugu*, which involves the practice of ancestral spirit worship, are important reminders of their cultural heritage. Modern Garifuna culture is responsible for the creation of Belize's only modern indigenous musical form, "Punta Rock." And every November there is a re-enactment of the first Garifuna arrival, a cause for widespread celebration and a reaffirmation of Garifuna identity within Belize.

Dugu

"The Dugu is performed following a request made by a deceased ancestor. The requests are made known in a ceremony previously held by the Buyae; this particular ceremony is called *Arairaguni* (bringing down). In this rite, the Buyae calls upon *hiuruha* (spirit helpers) to explain a particular problem. A family having gone through a series of misfortunes including sickness and death, will consult with the Buyae.

The Buyae in the Arairaguni ceremony, along with the hiuruha acts as a medium between a representative of the ill-fated family and Gubida – the deceased ancestors. There and then, the deceased ancestors make their desire known – for example, it may be that a great grandfather having been slighted by his delinquent grandchildren or children, has visited them with their misfortune. As a result, he requests a three-day Dugu. Preparations for this rite takes three main parts: 1. Invitation of relatives and friends from home and abroad, Belize, Guatemala, Honduras and U.S.A. 2. Food and drinks acquired; and specific efforts are made to obtain that particular food or drink which may be requested by the ancestor. 3. A date is agreed upon with the Buyae.

The primary purpose of the Dugu is the placating or appeasement of the Gubida Ancestors, on whose behalf it is being held. The Gubida is endowed with human qualities for the duration of the Dugu by all those participating. The ancestor may invite other Gubida to the feast. The Ancestor Spirit is asked to drink, eat and dance as he wishes. At tense moments during the ceremonies, one or more of the participants may lose consciousness, and in a trance called *Owohani* assume the characteristics of the Gubida Ancestor being honored.

At the end of the ceremonies, the ancestor is asked whether he acknowledges receipt of the Dugu. Depending on what he says, the ceremonies may have to be repeated."

Sebastien and Fabian Cayetano, *Belizean Garifuna Writers*

Politically and economically the Garifuna are influential in their own communities, but they are a minority ethnic group and their overall influence in Belize is no greater than that of the Maya. The influence of the Garifuna is also lessened by an emerging mestizo population in the South, and by external cultural forces that are beginning to disrupt the traditional Garifuna lifestyle.

The Mennonites

The two Mennonite groups in Belize, modernists (*Kleine Gemeinde*) and traditionalists (Old Colony), have made an enormous impact in the past 40 years, mainly through their skills as agriculturists. They are now an intrinsic part of the Belizean landscape and economy, particularly in the west of the country. Traditionally dressed Mennonites, the men with their long beards, straw hats, plain blue or green shirts, and dark gray trousers, and women wearing long floral print dresses and headscarves, travelling in one-horse carts are a common sight along the Western Highway.

The Mennonite church was started in Holland in the sixteenth century by a former Roman Catholic priest, Menno Simons, as a reaction against the deepening relationship between church and state. Mennonites are pacifists who run their own church-based communities. At the first sign of intent by the state to interfere in the running of Mennonite affairs, these communities are quite willing to migrate to a more welcoming environment—from Holland to Prussia, to Russia, to the U.S. and Canada, and to Mexico and Paraguay. Belize received its first Mennonite contingent in 1958 when a group of Mennonites from Mexico emigrated to Belize, settling in two locations: Blue Creek in the Orange Walk District and Spanish Lookout in the Cayo District.

Now, 40 years later, the Mennonites have settled throughout Belize, and new colonies are continually being established. Mennonite-run poultry, dairy and crop production provides much of Belize's chicken, milk and corn. Although the Mennonite community keeps largely to itself, there is a degree of integration, particularly in the Cayo District, where some Mennonites have moved away from their colony and some mainly Hispanic immigrants have joined Mennonite congregations. The success of the Mennonite farmers has caused some resentment among Belizeans, who allege questionable business and labor practices. Mennonites are accused of artificially driving prices down to stifle competition and of employing mainly non-unionized immigrant labor.

Religion

The Catholic Church came to assume its central role in Belize after the immigration of Yucatecan refugees from the Caste War, and European Jesuits began arriving in Belize in 1851 to attend to the new immigrants. In 1894 responsibility for the work of the Jesuits in Belize was transferred from the English Province of the Jesuit order to the Missouri Province in the U.S.

Church involvement in the provision of social services in the colony was welcome as it took away this responsibility from the settlers who were loath to invest in anything that did not yield a profit. Soon the church was running most of the educational establishments in the country, as well as health facilities and other socially oriented activities, including the credit unions.

The Jesuits' mission of evangelizing in Belize's towns and villages brought the Catholic faith to some of the most remote communities in Belize. Jesuit control of the education system, most notably the primary schools, continues today, and the order also runs the most prestigious educational establishment in the country, St. John's College in Belize City. Alongside the Jesuits, various orders of nuns work to promote the Catholic faith, most notably the Sisters of Mercy and the Pallotine Sisters.

Other Christian churches, including Anglican, Baptist and Methodist, are also very active, especially among the Creoles and the Garifuna, while in the newer Central American immigrant communities, evangelical

Mennonite men, Barton Creek   *Alain le Garsmeur/PANOS Pictures*

churches are popular. Because of Belize's proximity to the U.S., there are regular evangelizing missions from various Christian denominations operating throughout Belize.

Art, Music and Literature

While Belize has a rich cultural tradition, the introduction of cable television in the 1980s and the low priority given by the government to the arts has led to a depressingly flat and inactive national arts scene. There is nothing like the vibrancy one might expect from Belize's melting pot of cultures, and with limited national resources being stretched to provide basic services and infrastructure, the arts community has a real struggle. Nevertheless, there are plenty of talented Belizean artists, and enough enthusiastic supporters of the arts to enable some people to begin talking about a cultural revival in Belize.

The signs of this revival are coming from a number of directions. The government-run Arts Council is becoming more prominent in its support for the arts, and has recently attracted international funding to assist with its training and outreach program. It has also, since 1992, been promoting a showcase National Children's Festival of Arts every May. This takes place throughout the country, and gives Belize's young artists a stage on which to display their talents. There is also a National Dance Company that was formed in 1991, and plans are underway to establish a National Youth Choir and National Youth Band.

The local radio stations reflect the meeting of Caribbean and Latin cultures, playing mainly Jamaican bashment, reggae and dancehall, Trinidadian soca and calypso, and Latin music such as salsa and rancheros. For the most part, music in Belize is borrowed from the outside and most musicians survive by playing current favorites at local dances.

The regular appearance during the annual September celebrations of the veteran Jamaican showband Byron Lee and the Dragonaires, who are themselves adept at borrowing others' ideas, does nothing for the local music scene. Byron Lee songs and dances performed during his annual stint in Belize become the popular favorites for the coming year, forcing local musicians to concentrate on learning these to please the crowd.

Despite the obstacles, there is an emerging local recording industry, led by Stonetree Records from Benque Viejo. This industry is based on the international success of Belize's own Punta Rock musical style, spearheaded by Andy Palacio and Chico Ramos. This fast and energetic dance music has its roots in the Garifuna culture and has been given a positive reception in the U.S. and Europe. Stonetree Records has also released several albums of more traditional local music, including brukdown, traditional Garifuna drumming and Maya harp. There are also plans to introduce more local music into local radio programming.

Writers and Artists

Literature is undoubtedly the most developed area of Belizean culture. There are two local publishing houses, the Angelus Press and Cubola, that are both active in producing and promoting local writers. And internationally acclaimed Belizean writers such as Zoila Ellis and Zee Edgell, are part of a wider Caribbean literary tradition. Other popular local writers include the self-proclaimed voice of Belize's black underclass, Evan X Hyde, and David Ruiga, who writes in Spanish.

Belizean theater, which never appears to have been particularly strong despite the success of groups like the Square Peg Players, was dealt a body blow by the introduction of cable TV. Despite this, regular shows are put on at the Bliss Institute, Belize's only theatre and arts center built specifically for that purpose. Unfortunately, the Belize City location of the Bliss, its relatively high ticket prices, limited number of seats, and up-market type of performances mitigate against attracting "ordinary" Belizeans.

Local artists have found a very active and enthusiastic supporter in Yasser Musa, whose "Image Factory" gallery has become a focus for the visual arts. Regular promotions and events keep Belizean artists in the public eye. Among the most popular exhibits is Musa's own Belize City Poem, a personal video tour of Musa's hometown.

Newspapers, Politics and Personalities

Two of the nation's newspapers are produced by Belize's main political parties: the *Belize Times* by the People's United Party, and the *People's Pulse* by the United Democratic Party. Both concentrate on personal attacks on opposition politicians and contribute little to journalism or informed political debate. The two other newspapers, the *Reporter* and the *Amandala*, are more independent, but also suffer from the influence of partisan politics and personalities.

Amandala, for example, is owned and edited by Evan X Hyde, who in the 1960s formed the United Black Association for Development (UBAD), Belize's own "black power" party. The paper reflects his personal obsessions, which revolve around the historical trials and tribulations of UBAD, semi-professional basketball and homophobia. Despite the repetitive subject matter and the idiosyncratic reporting, Amandala remains Belize's most popular and entertaining newspaper.

From the Publisher

"A British reporter once asked Mahatma Gandhi the following question: 'What do you think of Western civilization?' The Mahatma thought briefly, then said in a measured tone, 'I think it would be a good idea.'

At AMANDALA, the leading newspaper in Belize since 1981, we think the time is right for us to inform or remind, whichever is appropriate, that the mandate of the newly elected government, the largest mandate in the last 30 years, includes the directive to teach African and indigenous Indian history in the schools of Belize. This is something that the local Jesuits should now initiate and promote on their own, without state insistence. After all, in their schools in North America, they have to teach these things. Why should the schools in Central America be different?

The jig's up, so to speak. For 500 years, Eurocentric educators tried to convince us that Columbus 'discovered' us while trying to have us believe that they civilized us. No, they Christianized us in Africa and America, but they did not civilize us. Civilization is what barbarian European pirates met when they first visited Africa and America.

And talking about Christianity? Who do you think killed six million Jews in Nazi Germany? Who do you think killed 100 million Africans in the slave trade? Who do you think dropped atomic bombs on Hiroshima and Nagasaki? And who's bombing little children in Northern Ireland?

The issue today, however, is not religion. It is education. At a certain point in history, roughly 500 years ago, Europe 'met' Africa and America. By force of arms, Europe subjugated Africa and America, imposed its administrations and religions, and raped the civilizations of these conquered continents. Good for Europe. There were battles and wars, and Europe won. The issue of civilizing Africans and indigenous Americans, however, is now a manifest non-starter in academic circles.

Europe had no civilization before she met Africa and America. It was Islamic Moors who civilized Spain between the ninth and fifteenth centuries A.D.

There were practices and traditions in both Africa and America that we Africans and Americans today consider backward or brutal. No lie. But too many generations of Africans and Americans grew up in the so-called New World being brainwashed by a European educational system which taught us that our ancestors were good for nothing, and that our people were 'saved' by the penetration/conquest of our societies/continents by enlightened Europeans. That is a lie. Straight. It's a damned lie.

So listen up, Jesuitiques. Try to get it straight. That's part of what the people of Belize voted for on August 27 (1998). And this is a sovereign nation; or have you forgotten September 21, 1981? Sovereign nation, sovereign will. Educate. Don't obfuscate."

Evan X Hyde, Editor, *Amandala*, October 1998

Hyde also runs the most popular radio station, Radio Krem, which has survived efforts by successive governments to close it down. One of Krem's biggest draws has been its Dickie Bradley phone-in show. Bradley, a lawyer by profession, also hosts *One-on-One*, a weekly TV discussion show (and one of the very few Belizean-produced TV shows). He is probably the closest Belize gets to investigative journalism and the irreverent and inquiring nature of his interviews makes him the most popular media personality. His new role as a senator and PUP government minister may well mean that Belize loses its best home-grown journalistic talent.

Cable Television

While radio remains the most popular medium of mass communication, many homes in Belize, even in rural areas, now have a television, and an increasing number have access to cable television, which is relayed from the U.S. In Belize City, for example, people have access to about 60 channels, which include religion, sports, news, music and feature films.

This phenomenon, which started in the 1980s, has dramatically increased the impact of American culture on Belizean life. Many are quick to blame imported TV shows for the growth in violent crime, especially in Belize City. As well as contributing to an increase in the acceptance of violence among young people, the influence of so much imported culture on the local arts scene has been entirely negative, according to writers and artists. It is only recently that Belize's politicians have seemed to acknowledge the importance of culture in shaping a society, and while a ban on imported cable TV is unlikely, a more active promotion of local arts would give Belizeans an opportunity to better develop and define their own identity.

WHERE TO GO, WHAT TO SEE

Reef, Ruins and Rainforest

Unlike much of the rest of the Caribbean and Central America, Belize has not gone the way of large-scale resort development. A visit to Belize is instead a more individually tailored experience, with three main attractions – the three R's of reef, ruins and rainforest. Most package vacations to Belize include an element of each of these: usually a few days on the cayes followed by a brief stay in a jungle lodge exploring the forest and visiting Mayan ruins. While these are the essentials, there are other activities that should really be part of everyone's Belizean experience.

Belize City

Most people, acting on first impressions and second-hand reports, choose to avoid Belize City altogether, which is a shame as it is worth getting to know. The city is surprisingly small and easy to get around. It is built on two sides of the Belize River and can be entered in one of two directions, either along the Northern Highway or the Western Highway. The city is surrounded by the Caribbean Sea, and the areas around Battlefield Park, Baron Bliss Lighthouse and the south side of the Belize River near the Governor's House are particularly picturesque. Probably the most convenient way of seeing the city is to take the daily open top tour bus, which gives a brief history of all the places of interest.

The Belize Zoo

A good starting point for any visitor wanting to experience Belize's wildlife is the Belize Zoo, 29 miles west of Belize City. The brainchild of Sharon Matola, who took over the care of some animals abandoned after the budget of a wildlife film was cut, the zoo has a reputation for being more animal-centered than most such attractions. It plays a big part in educating Belizean children about their country's wildlife, especially through the Tropical Education Center just across the road from the zoo, which has accommodation and classroom facilities.

Crooked Tree

For birdwatchers, Belize is paradise. Crooked Tree Wildlife Sanctuary, about 30 miles north of Belize City, is an extensive wetlands habitat that includes several lagoons and rivers and boasts hundreds of species of birds. Crooked Tree is also the largest of several traditional rural Creole villages in this area and is a fascinating place to visit for people wanting to learn about Creole culture.

Bermudian Landing

Another traditional Creole village is the home of the Community Baboon Sanctuary at Bermudian Landing. Known as baboons in Belize, these animals are more commonly known as Central American Black Howler Monkeys and are an endangered species in the region. The project relies almost entirely on donations and the voluntary support of local Creole subsistence farmers who allow their private lands to be set aside as a protected habitat for the Howlers. The success of the project can be seen by the size of the Howler population in the area, which has grown to over 1,800.

Lamanai and Altun Ha

In the same area as Crooked Tree are two Mayan sites worth a visit. A visit to Lamanai (translated as either "Submerged Crocodile" or "Drowned Insect") combines a beautiful river trip along the New River with one of the most fascinating Mayan ruins. There is also a museum of Mayan artifacts on site. Altun Ha (Water of the Rock), 33 miles up the Maskall Road (the old Northern Highway) was an important Mayan ceremonial and trading center and it was here that the Jade Head of Kinich Ahau, the Mayan Sun God, was found.

Western Belize
Accommodation and Activities

Cayo is the most developed tourist destination inland. It is possible to stay fairly cheaply in a basic budget hotel in the town of San Ignacio (also called Cayo by the locals) or more expensively in one of the cabaña style resorts in the surrounding hills. Resort prices vary significantly and prices are most often quoted in US$, which are twice the prices quoted in B$, so be careful. It is also possible to stay in the Mountain Pine Ridge, which is a unique experience, although high transportation and accommodation costs make this an alternative for the wealthier traveler only.

In general, budget travelers find accommodation in Belize hard to come by. St. Ignacio is one of the few places that caters to tourists not in possession of a gold credit card. Activities in and around St. Ignacio include canoeing along one of the Macal or Mopan rivers, horseback riding, jungle hikes and caving. St. Ignacio is also a good base for exploring; Caracol and the whole Mountain Pine Ridge area and Tikal in Guatemala, are both within reach, although transportation can be expensive.

Mayan Sites

The newly discovered Caracol (Spanish for "snail") was one of the Maya world's largest cities. Still under extensive excavation, it rivals Tikal, which it once dominated, for size and importance, and contains Caana ("sky palace"), the tallest Maya building in Belize.

Two smaller Mayan ruins are in easy reach of St. Ignacio. Xunantunich (Maiden of the Rock) includes the spectacular El Castillo building and involves crossing the Mopan River on a hand-winched car ferry. Cahal Pech (Place of the Ticks), in St. Ignacio itself, is a more modest Mayan site, without the imposing temple structures, and as a result gives the impression of being very much more human.

Heading South
Dangriga and Hopkins

The Hummingbird Highway is almost a destination in itself. This newly-paved road weaves through the lush forest-covered Mayan Mountains before descending into the Stann Creek Valley. The end of the road is Dangriga Town, the capital of Belize's Garifuna community. Dangriga can be an acquired taste, as, like Belize City, it is busy, hot and not particularly interested in tourists. However, Garifuna are among the most genuine and friendly people in the world (though new visitors can expect some hassle from a few rent-a-dreads who are usually stoned on marijuana or crack). Perhaps the best way to experience Garifuna culture is to travel a few miles further on, down the Southern Highway (which starts before Dangriga Town) and turn off to Hopkins Village. The Southern Highway is Belize's last unpaved major highway and can make for an arduous journey, especially during the dry season, when the dust can be unbearable.

Hopkins is a recommended stop for those who enjoy the beach life but are also interested in learning more about Garifuna culture. Particularly recommended is the Sandy Beach Lodge, a beachfront guesthouse run by Garifuna women. This place is only for those seeking comfort and peace. Near Hopkins is the Cockscomb Basin Wildlife Preserve, one of the world's very few jaguar reserves. Here it is possible to take a walk through the jungle in search of jaguar paw prints, although jaguars are only rarely seen as they are nocturnal and shy animals.

Maya Guesthouse Program

The Maya Guesthouse Program, based in the hill villages further south in the Toledo District, gives visitors the chance to live in a traditional Mayan village. This is a unique opportunity for the tourist to experience Maya culture and to explore one of the world's most beautiful and fascinating landscapes. It also gives the Maya community an opportunity to share in the income derived from tourism, while at the same time promoting their culture and lifestyle to the outside world.

Punta Gorda

The southernmost town of Punta Gorda is a good base for exploring, and accommodation here can be found quite reasonably since tourism is new to the area and so facilities remain fairly basic. Road and trail travel can also be difficult in the rainy season. It is possible to take a boat from here to head off to explore the Garifuna town of Livingstone and the beautiful Rio Dulce, both in Guatemala. Bicycles are also available for rent and can be a good way to get to see the surrounding countryside.

There are three Mayan sites in the Toledo District, which can be reached from Punta Gorda – Lubaantun (Place of the Fallen Rocks), Nim Li Punit (Big Hat) and Uxbenka (the Old Place). The latter two were only discovered in 1976 and 1984 respectively and had already suffered from extensive looting. Nim Li Punit includes the tallest (31 feet) carved stone monument in Belize and interesting hieroglyphics and carvings on its ceremonial stones and stelae. Uxbenka has suffered badly from erosion and no restoration work has yet been carried out.

The Crystal Skull

Lubaantun is unusual as it was constructed from crystalline limestone blocks with no visible mortar, and some buildings and carvings which would have been made from stone at other Mayan sites were made from perishable materials such as wood and palm fronds. The best-known discovery at Lubantuun is the Crystal Skull, which was unearthed in 1926 by Anna Mitchell-Hedges (daughter of the archeologist F.A. Mitchell-Hedges) on her seventeenth birthday. The Crystal Skull was carved from an 8-inch cube of pure rock crystal and shows virtually no tool marks. Some believe the discovery to have been a hoax, while others think it is linked to the lost continent of Atlantis.

Out to Sea
Underwater World

Belize's reef offers some of the best diving in the world, and Belize has become an internationally renowned diving destination. Many visitors spend almost no time on the mainland, choosing to head straight to hotels on the cayes or to live-aboard boats. Belize offers exhilarating diving for experienced and inexperienced alike. Non-divers can learn to dive as part of their vacation or can instead enjoy some quite wonderful snorkeling or tour over the reef in a glass bottom boat.

Ambergris and Caye Caulker

Ambergris Caye is Belize's most popular and most developed caye and the closest Belize gets to package tourism. Even so, it is still very relaxed and

Half Moon Caye   *James Beveridge*

a very enjoyable place to visit. Caye Caulker is quieter (but developing quickly) and offers more in the way of budget accommodation. Both can be reached in under an hour from Belize City by water taxi or in a few minutes by plane. While the beaches do not match up to those found in other Caribbean destinations, the friendly atmosphere and the opportunities for diving and snorkeling are unparalleled. The most popular destination for day trips is the Hol Chan Marine Reserve. Hol Chan includes the spectacular Boca Ciego, a collapsed cave with an underwater freshwater spring that literally teems with fish.

Placencia, the Southern Cayes and Further Afield

In the south the Placencia peninsula is growing in popularity and is a good base from which to explore the Southern Cayes. At the extreme southern end of the peninsula, Placencia Village is a small fishing-turned tourism village that offers good accommodation, some of Belize's best beaches, and easy access to the relatively unspoiled Southern Cayes. Further up the peninsula, around Seine Beight, there are a growing number of up-market foreign-owned resorts that can tend to be a little exclusive, especially given Belize's reputation for being relaxed and welcoming.

The larger Southern Cayes are increasingly being developed for up-market tourism or for scientific research. It is possible to take day trips out to some of the smaller Southern Cayes from Placencia or Dangriga, and a recommended destination is the popular Laughing Bird Caye. This area is a Marine Reserve and probably takes its name from the happiness of the pelicans who feast on the bountiful fish around the Caye. More difficult to arrange but well worth the extra effort are trips to one of the three atolls: Lighthouse Reef, Glover's Reef and the Turneffe Islands, all of which offer an even greater variety and abundance of marine life.

The Blue Hole

Beside Lighthouse Reef is the Blue Hole National Park. The Blue Hole is an almost perfectly circular limestone sinkhole more than 300 feet across and 400 feet deep, which was created by the collapse of an underwater cavern some 12,000 years ago. In 1984 the underwater explorer, Jacques Cousteau, made a documentary film about the Blue Hole and concluded that a network of caves and crevices extends beneath the entire reef. Divers can admire outstanding stalagmite and stalactite formations, although big fish have trouble finding their way in because of the shallow surrounding waters.

On the Buses

Belize's bus service is cheap, reliable and has to be the best way to get to know the country. While the buses may not be the most luxurious (though on Express routes they're not at all bad), if it's real Belize you're after, a trip by bus is unbeatable. Highly recommended are Novelo's and Batty's, which both operate from terminals in Belize City.

Two bus trips worth doing are to Chetumal just over the border in Mexico, and to Melchor, the Guatemalan border town on the western border. To get to Chetumal from Belize City involves travelling the entire length of the Northern Highway, passing through the wetlands and sugar cane fields, before arriving at the usually busy border crossing. Chetumal has boomed since its promotion as a business zone, and many Belizeans cross the border in search of bargains, homing in on the modern, well-stocked, San Francisco de Assisi supermarket. In 1995, when the peseta devalued dramatically, the border was clogged with Belizeans, as prices in Chetumal were one-third of Belizean prices. Despite some leveling off of prices, Chetumal remains popular with Belizeans and visitors and is still cheap.

The Melchor trip takes you from Belize City the entire length of the Western Highway, past St. Ignacio and Benque Viejo. Melchor is popular with Belizeans, but is a different prospect, being a smaller rather run-down market town. Its main attraction for visitors are the handmade crafts sold in many of the shops. Hammocks, clothes and carvings can be bought here at prices far below those on the Belizean market.

TIPS FOR TRAVELERS

Safety

Belize is fairly safe, provided that common sense precautions are taken. The biggest danger you face will be petty theft, so do what you can to minimize this threat.

• While most all of Belize (including Belize City) is safe during the day, try to steer clear of out of the way places, especially if you're walking alone.
• At night exercise more precautions. If you want to go for a walk, take someone else along with you, and ask someone knowledgeable (a taxi driver or hotel receptionist) if they think it is safe. It is probably best to avoid walking anywhere after nine p.m. in Belize City. Also, some petty thieves target areas close to the larger hotels, so be especially careful walking close by any of these.
• Do not carry or wear valuables – jewelry, watches, cash – with you unless absolutely necessary.

You will also undoubtedly be "hassled" at some point for "a dollar to buy some bread" or with an offer of unspecified service – "how you doin' man, how can I help you?" A polite "no thank you" will end most encounters, although it is often just as easy to give the requested dollar.

It is advisable, if you intend to travel by car, especially if you're venturing off the main highways to carry plenty of water, not to pick up hitchhikers, and to have someone know when you are expected to arrive at your destination.

Travel

Most people arrive in Belize via Miami (TACA or American Airlines) or Houston (Continental Airlines). There is also a direct New Orleans-Belize flight with TACA. There are currently no direct flights from Europe, although it is possible that these will be available in the near future once improvements to Belize's airport are completed. It is also possible to enter Belize by air from Mexico and Central America – TACA serves Guatemala City, San José, Panama City, San Pedro Sula, and San Salvador. Aviateca also serves Guatemala City. Regular domestic air services link most of the major towns and cayes; there are eleven municipal airstrips and two domestic air carriers – Maya Island Air and Tropic Air. It is also possible to charter planes from one of several smaller companies.

Road travelers can enter Belize through Mexico at Belize's northern border at Chetumal/Corozal Town or Guatemala via the western border at

Melchor/Benque Viejo. There are also regular sea crossings available between Guatemala (Puerto Barrios) and Honduras (Puerto Cortez) and Punta Gorda Town in the south of Belize.

A good travel service is available to the cayes from Belize's mainland by plane or boat. The inland bus service is also very good. Car rental is possible, but expensive, because it is essential to have 4-wheel drive unless you know you won't be veering off the main paved roads.

Health

In general Belize is a safe place to visit so long as some care is taken. If you will be travelling inland, it is wise to take precautions against malaria, which is a problem especially in the south and west of the country. If travelling outside the main towns, you should stick to bottled water (which is readily available) and always make sure you have enough water to drink regularly in order to avoid dehydration. Sunburn can be avoided by staying out of the sun during the hottest times of the day (11 am to 2 pm) and by using the correct factor sun lotion or sun block.

The reef and forests can also present health risks to the inexperienced. If out on the reef, take care not to touch the coral as not only is it very delicate, but some coral can also cause skin rashes and worse. The same is true for the forest. Some trees and plants are dangerous to touch, so either only go into the forest with an experienced guide or make sure you check what to avoid with someone beforehand.

Belize is also home to a number of dangerous insects and animals. The most common and annoying are the mosquito, battlass fly and sandfly. While not particularly dangerous (except in the case of a malaria-carrying mosquito), these insects swarm at dawn and dusk and can leave their victim covered in very itchy bites. To avoid being bitten, use an insect repellent, wear long sleeves, long trousers and socks at dawn and dusk, and use a mosquito net or stay somewhere where the windows and doors have mosquito screens fitted.

Other common dangers are tarantulas, scorpions and snakes, all of which can give painful bites, but which are only likely to be encountered by those straying off the beaten track.

Changing Money

The Belize dollar (B$) is fixed to the U.S.$ at a rate of U.S.$1 = B$2, and because of this U.S.$ are widely accepted as an unofficial second currency. Banks and many other business establishments give the official bank selling rate for B$ which is U.S.$1 = B$1.9825. Banks will also accept most major currencies. There is also an unofficial ("gray") market in U.S.$ due to a seasonal shortage of foreign exchange in the economy. At certain times of the year, such as around Christmas, the unofficial rate can reach U.S.$1 = B$ 2.1.

Visitors should be aware that prices in Belize do tend to be on the high side and certainly nowhere near as cheap as in Mexico or other Central American countries.

Souvenirs

Belize has been slow to produce its own range of crafts and souvenirs. Most are imported from neighboring Mexico or Guatemala, where costs of production are lower and there is an already developed industry. For this reason many tourists prefer to buy their gifts in the border towns of Chetumal in Mexico, or in Melchor, Guatemala, where there is more choice and the price is generally much lower. Belize does produce its own slate and wood carvings, and there are signs that local crafts people may be becoming better organized to produce a more authentically Belizean range of keepsakes.

Drugs

Belize produces marijuana and is also an important transshipment point for the Colombian cocaine trade. As a result, these drugs are readily available in Belize, but as their possession and use are illegal it is highly recommended that they be avoided.

Time

Belize is six hours behind GMT and one hour behind EST.

ADDRESSES AND CONTACTS

Belize Tourism Industry Association
Box 62
10 North Park Street
Belize City
Tel.: 501 2 75717   Fax: 501 2 78710
E-mail: btia@btl.net

Belize Tourist Board
Box 325, 83 North Front Street
Belize City
Tel.: 501 2 77213/73255
Fax: 501 2 77490

Cubola Productions / Stonetree Records
Benque Viejo Del Carmen
Cayo District
Tel.: 501 9 32083   Fax: 501 9 32240
E-mail: cubolabz@btl.net

Society for the Promotion of Education
and Research (SPEAR)
34 Freetown Road
Belize City
Tel. 501 2 31668
E-mail: spear@btl.net

Association of National Development
Agencies (ANDA)
34 Freetown Road
Belize City
Tel.: 501 2 35115
E-mail: anda@btl.net

Belize Audubon Society
29 Regent Street
Belize City
Tel.: 501 2 77369
E-mail: bas@btl.net

Belize Chamber of Commerce and
Industry
P.O. Box 291
6 Church Street
Belize City
Tel.: 501 2 74394   Fax: 501 2 74984
E-mail: chamber@btl.net

Belize on the Web
There are now hundreds of Belize web
sites. The ones listed below are among the
best on offer and a good starting point for
further exploration.

Belize by Naturalight (http://
www.belizenet.com)

You Better Belize It (http://
www.belizeit.com)

Belize Tourist Board (http://
www.turq.com/belize.html)

Lonely Planet—Destination Belize (http:/
/www.lonelyplanet.com/dest/cam/
belize.htm/)

Amandala On-Line (http://
belizemall.com/amandala/)

FURTHER READING AND BOOKSTORES

Travel Guides
Mahler, R. and Wotkyns, S., *Belize: A Natural Destination*. New Mexico, 1995.
Whatmore, M. and Eltringham, P., *The Rough Guide to Guatemala and Belize*. London, updated
    regularly.

Non-Fiction
Ashcraft, N., *Colonialism and Underdevelopment*. New York, 1973.
Arvigo, R. & Epstein, N., *Sastun: My Apprenticeship with a Maya Healer*. London, 1994.
Barry, T., *Inside Belize*. Albuquerque, 1992.
Bolland, O.N., *Belize: A New Nation in Central America*. Boulder CO, 1986.
Foster, B., *Spirit Possession in the Garifuna Community of Belize*. Belize, 1994 (2nd ed.).
Foster, B., *Warlords and Maize Men: A Guide to the Maya Sites of Belize*. Belize, 1989.
Grant, C.H., *The Making of Modern Belize*. Cambridge, 1976.
Hyde, E. X, *X-Communication*. Belize, 1995.
King, E., *Belize 1798: The Road to Glory: The Battle of St George's Caye*. Belize, 1991.
Shoman, A., *XIII Chapters of A History of Belize*. Belize, 1994.
Shoman, A. & MacPherson, A.S. (ed.), *Backtalking Belize: Selected Writings*. Belize, 1995.
Stevens, K., *Jungle Walk: Birds and Beasts of Belize*. Belize, 1989.
Young, C.N., *Creole Proverbs of Belize*. 1988.

Fiction and Poetry
Anderson, H.W., *The Son of Kinich: Illustrated Poetical Works*. Belize, 1995.
Edgell, Z., *In Times Like These*. Belize.
Edgell, Z., *Beka Lamb*. London, 1982.
Ellis, Z., *On Heroes, Lizards and Passion*. Belize
Lindo, L., *Tales of the Belizean Woods*. Belize, 1995.
Musa, Y., Shoman, K. and Waight S., *Shots from the Heart: Three Young Belizean Poets*. Belize,
    1995
Phillips, M. (ed.), *Snapshots of Belize: An Anthology of Short Fiction*. Belize, 1995.
Phillips, M. (ed.), *Ping Wing Juk Me: Six Belizean Plays*. Belize, 1996.
Ruiz Puga, D. N., *Old Benque*. Belize, 1990.
Young, C.N., *Pataki Full: Seven Belizean Short Stories*. Belize, 1997 (4th ed.).

Local Bookstores

Book Centre	Belize Bookshop	The Book Shop
2 Church Street	Regent Street	126 Freetown Road
Belize City	Belize City	Belize City

FACTS AND FIGURES

GEOGRAPHY

Official name: Belize
Situation: Belize is on the Caribbean coast of Central America. To the north lies Mexico's Yucatán peninsula and to the west and south lie Guatemala and the Gulf of Honduras. Due east of Belize lie the islands of Jamaica and Cuba, which mark the beginning of the Caribbean island chain, and northeast lie the Florida Keys, the southernmost tip of the U.S. Belize is the only English speaking country in Central America, and its borders were carved out in the eighteenth century in negotiations between Britain and Spain that established the Belize mainland as extending 174 miles (280km) from the Rio Hondo River in the north (the border with Mexico) to the Sarstoon River in the south (the border with Guatemala). At its widest point Belize measures 68 miles (109 km), from the Caribbean coast to the western border with Guatemala.
Surface area: 8,867 sq. miles (22,962 sq. km). Belize is double the size of Jamaica, or slightly larger than El Salvador, which have populations of three million and eight million respectively. In a regional context, the Central American isthmus has a total land area of 201,930 sq. miles (523,000 sq. km) and a population of approximately 31.3 million (1993). The average Central American population density is 155 per sq. mile (60 per sq. km), or some six times that of Belize. Belize's estimated population of 221,120 (1996) gives it an extremely low population density of about 25 people per square mile (10 per sq. km.). The abundance of land in Belize, even if it is not all productive, still attracts a regular flow of immigrants from the neighboring republics.

Administrative division: There are six administrative districts: Belize, Cayo, Corozal, Orange Walk, Stann Creek and Toledo.
Capital: The official capital is Belmopan, pop. 6,000 (1997 est.), although the commercial capital remains Belize City.
Other principal cities (with populations): Belize City, 70,000; Orange Walk, 12,000; Corozal Town, 7,500; St. Ignacio, 8,000; Dangriga Town, 8,000; Punta Gorda, 4,000; San Pedro (Ambergris Caye), 1,700; Caye Caulker, 800.
Infrastructure: four main highways: Northern (96 miles) and Western (82 miles), both paved, Hummingbird (54 miles) and Southern (93 miles) partly paved and due to be completed under ongoing projects.

The Coastal Highway (36 miles) links mile 31 (from Belize City) on the Western Highway with mile 11 (from Dangriga Town) on the Hummingbird Highway. This is a dirt road and is often closed due to flooding. Philip Goldson International Airport, nine miles north of Belize City, is main airport. There is a municipal airport in King's Park area of Belize City and fifteen rural airstrips. There are sea ports in Belize City and Big Creek.
Relief and landscape: The land area is usually divided into four distinct geographical areas: the northern area, which is mainly flat plain; the Maya Mountains, which dominate the central and western area of the country; the south, with its more varied topography and wetter climate; and, finally, the offshore. Most of northern Belize is a low flat plain, with mangrove swamps and marshes near the coastline. This plain is fed by slow-moving rivers flowing down from the shallow slopes of the limestone hills in the west. The Rio Hondo and New Rivers run into Corozal Bay, while closer to Belize City, the Northern, Belize, and Sibun rivers empty into the channels between the mainland and the Barrier Reef. The sedimen-

tary deposits from these rivers have created a swampy coastal area. There are also several large shallow fresh water and brackish water lagoons along the coast. The largest of these, the Northern and Southern Lagoons, lie a short distance south of Belize City.

The Maya Mountains that dominate southern central Belize make a welcome change from the monotony of the flat plains in the north. They are covered with mixed hardwood forests and rise to 3,699 feet (1,110 meters) at Victoria Peak, whose dark quartz-covered summit dominates the landscape. This is part of the oldest land surface in Central America, the four million-year old Mountain Pine Ridge, which was once part of an ancient island.

The south of Belize lies on the southern boundary of the North American Plate, a tectonic plate that stretches all the way from Alaska. Poor roads and an inhospitable climate have in the past made this part of Belize's territory suitable only for the brave and/or foolhardy. But gradually over the past few years, road and internal air transportation have improved. Continued improvements are coming as both international aid donors and the Belize government see the upgrading of Belize's southern infrastructure as essential for the development of the country. At present, despite being home to two of Belize's major export industries, citrus and bananas, road conditions in the region are poor and many villages in the south are without electricity and running water. The south is the most diverse region of Belize both in terms of landscape and people. South from Belmopan, the Hummingbird Highway weaves its way through the fertile foothills of the Maya Mountains. Mennonite and refugee homesteaders are taking advantage of the rich soils in this area, establishing new farming communities. This is undoubtedly one of the most beautiful parts of Belize, as the lush forest-covered Maya Mountains rise up majestically from the foothills.

Forty miles south from Belmopan, the highway emerges from the mountains and follows the low lying coastal belt. The Hummingbird Highway ends at the coastal town of Dangriga. Seven miles before Dangriga is the turnoff onto the Southern Highway that runs all the way to Belize's southernmost town of Punta Gorda. The southern Belizean rivers rise in the granite Maya Mountains, so the coastal soils in this part of the country tend to be sandy. While this is bad for agriculture, it is to the benefit of the tourism industry as it has created a number of good beaches, most notably at Hopkins and along the Placencia Peninsula. Both are becoming increasingly developed as tourist destinations, with Placencia in particular attracting large-scale foreign investment.

Inland from the agricultural belt are the hills and mountains of the Cockscomb Range and the southern slopes of the Maya Mountains. The southern hills are home to Belize's Ke'kchi and Mopan Maya, who live in remote dispersed village communities, and also to Belize's only true rainforest; significantly more rain falls in the south than the rest of the country.

Belize's coastline is 174 miles (280 km) in length, and its most significant feature is the Barrier Reef, which runs the entire length of the coast at a distance of 10 to 20 miles from the shore. The reef is the second longest in the world, after the Great Barrier Reef of Queensland, Australia (1,200 miles/1,930 km long). The reef is perhaps Belize's most valuable natural asset as it not only helps to protect the coast from the effects of hurricanes, but also plays a major role in the tourism and fishing industries. The United Nations has declared it a World Heritage Site, stating that any deterioration would represent a "harmful impoverishment of all nations of the world." In total it is estimated that Belize's offshore contains about 350 miles of coral reef and 280 square miles of island landmass. And as with a good deal of the interior of the country, a lot of this offshore territory is little explored.

Ambergris Caye and Caye Caulker are the most developed offshore territories and there are another twenty or so smaller cayes that have some form of development, either in the shape of tourism and/or research facilities or fishing camps. The other 200-odd cayes are for the most part undisturbed, with those in the south of the country, off the coast of Dangriga and Placencia, being the least visited.

Of Belize's three atolls – Turneffe Islands, Lighthouse Reef and Glovers Reef – the first is largest and nearest to the mainland, measuring 30 miles long and 10 miles across at its widest point and lying about 20 miles to the east of Belize City. Turneffe covers a total land area of 205 square miles, made up of an archipelago of 35 coral islets and mangrove ranges around a shallow lagoon, which is connected to the outer Caribbean waters by "bogues," openings between the mangrove thickets.

Lighthouse Reef, which lies 30 miles further to the east, is 28 miles long and 6 miles across at its widest. Its lagoon is almost completely surrounded by coral formations. Glovers Reef, the most remote of Belize's island groups, is 15 miles long by 5 miles wide, and lies to the south of Turneffe Islands and Lighthouse Reef, about 40 miles east of Dangriga Town.

Climate: Belize's climate is fairly mild. Coastal temperatures range from about 10°C / 50°F to 30°C / 95°F, although it can get cooler higher up in the Maya mountains, or hotter inland away from the cooling sea breezes. The country can, however, experience some of the heaviest rainfall in the world. Rainfall varies dramatically from north to south; the north's average annual rainfall of 51 inches (1.295m) is less than a third of the 175 inches (4.445m) that falls in the south. The main dry season extends from February to May and the wet season is June to October. There is also usually a short dry spell in August. From September until the end of November each year is the hurricane season.

Flora and fauna: Forest: 70%; land suitable for mechanized agriculture: 19%; land held in designated reserves (public and private): 32%; annual deforestation rate: 3-5%; flow-ering plants: 4,000 species; birds: 533 species (33 threatened); mammals: 155 species (15 threatened); reptiles: 107 species (7 threatened); native trees: 700 varieties; orchids: 72 varieties.

Both the inland and offshore are home to an extraordinary variety of birds, animals, plants, and marine life. Belize is home to birds such as toucans, parrots, blue-crowned motmots, red-footed boobies, jabiru storks, grackles, egrets, vireos, herons, pelicans, ospreys, hummingbirds, cuckoos, and magnificent frigate birds. Animals include jaguars, ocelots, tapirs, turtles, land crabs, boa constrictors, lizards, iguanas, frogs, opossums, raccoons, pacas and armadillos, and plants include mahogany, cohune and coconut palms, ficus trees, ziricote, gumbo-limbo, sea grape, spider lily and, of course, mangrove. The sea is teeming with life, with over 220 types of fish identified including squirrelfish, grey angels, parrot fish, horse-eye jacks, blue-striped grunts, barracuda, hogfish, tarpon, snook, grouper, bonefish, marlin and tuna as well as dolphins, sharks, spotted eagle rays, hermit crabs, sponges and purple cleaner shrimp.

POPULATION

Population (1996 est.): 221,120.
Annual population growth (1996 est.): 2.6%.
Urbanization (1996): 47%.
Fertility (1993): a Belizean woman has an average of 4.6 children.
Age structure (1991): 0-14: 44%; 15-64: 52%; 65+ 4%.
Birth rate (1997): 34 per 1,000 pop.
Mortality rate (1997): 6 per 1,000 pop.
Infant mortality (1996): 34 per 1,000 life births.
Average life expectancy: females: 71.8 years; males: 68.2 years.
Health care: 1 doctor per 1,562 inhabitants (1996); access to safe water 83% (1995); access to sanitation 39% (1995). There are 140 doctors, 300 nurses and 233 midwifes registered in Belize. There are 550 hospital beds located in 7 government hospitals – in Belize City, Belmopan, and each of the other main district towns. There are also 37 health centers and 35 rural health posts.
Illiteracy (1996): 7.6%.
Education: Government spends 17% of GDP on education. Primary education—8 years starting at age 5—is free and compulsory. Children completing primary education: 54% (1995). 280 primary schools (1996), of which churches administer over 80%. 31 secondary schools (1996), 8 institutions offering tertiary education (1996), including the University College of Belize (UCB). Also an adult education institute in Belize City, operated by the University of the West Indies, and a number of specialized vocational training institutions, including the Centres for Employment Training and the College of Agriculture as well as government youth training initiatives.
Social development index (UNDP Human Development Index 1996): 67 out of 174 countries ranked.
Ethnic composition (1996): mestizo 43.6%, Creole 29.8%, Maya 11.1%, Garifuna 6.6%, East Indian 3.5%, Mennonite 3.1%, other 2.2%.
Religion (1996): Roman Catholic 57.7%, Anglican 6.9%, Pentecostal 6.3%, Methodist 4.2%, Adventist 4.1%, Mennonite 4%, Nazarene 2.5%, Hindu 2.5%, Jehovah's Witness 1.4%, other/none 10.4%.
Languages: English (official), Creole English (most widely spoken), Spanish, Garifuna, Yucatec, Ke'kchi, Mopan, Low-German, Hindi .

HISTORY AND POLITICS

Key historical dates: 1200BC–AD250: Pre-Classic Maya civilization * AD 300–900: Classic Maya civilization * AD 900–1500: Post-Classic Maya civilization * 1508: first Spanish contact with Belize Maya * 1638: first settlement of British Baymen * 1787: name "British Honduras" first used * 1796/7: Garifuna deported from St. Vincent to Roatán by British * 1798: Battle of St. George's Caye establishes British military superiority in Belize * 1802: first recorded Garifuna settlement in Belize * 1802: Spain acknowledges British sovereignty over Belize in Treaty of Amiens * 1832: main Garifuna settlement of Belize * 1838: abolition of slavery * 1840s: Guerra de Castes/ Caste War in Yucatán * 1871: British Honduras becomes a British Crown Colony * 1954: universal adult suffrage introduced * 1958: arrival of Mennonites from Mexico * 1964: attainment of internal self-government * 1973: name changed to Belize / Belize is a founding member of Caricom * 1981: "Heads of Agreement" meeting in London sets out areas for future negotiation between Belize and Guatemala / Attainment

BELIZE

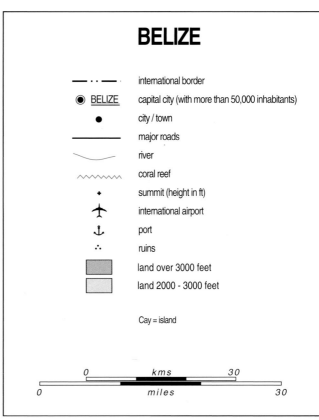

— ·· —	international border
⦿ <u>BELIZE</u>	capital city (with more than 50,000 inhabitants)
●	city / town
——	major roads
～	river
∿∿∿	coral reef
✛	summit (height in ft)
✈	international airport
⚓	port
∴	ruins
▓	land over 3000 feet
▢	land 2000 - 3000 feet

Cay = island

0	*k m s*	30
0	*miles*	30

UNITED STATES

● New Orleans

ATLANTIC OCEAN

MEXICO

Gulf of Mexico

BAHAMAS

● Miami

HAVANA ▣

● Mexico City

CUBA

● Guantánamo

CAYMAN ISLANDS (UK)

JAMAICA

BELIZE

GUATEMALA / HONDURAS

EL SALVADOR

NICARAGUA

CARIBBEAN SEA

PACIFIC OCEAN

Panama Canal

COSTA RICA

PANAMA

0	km	400
0	miles	400

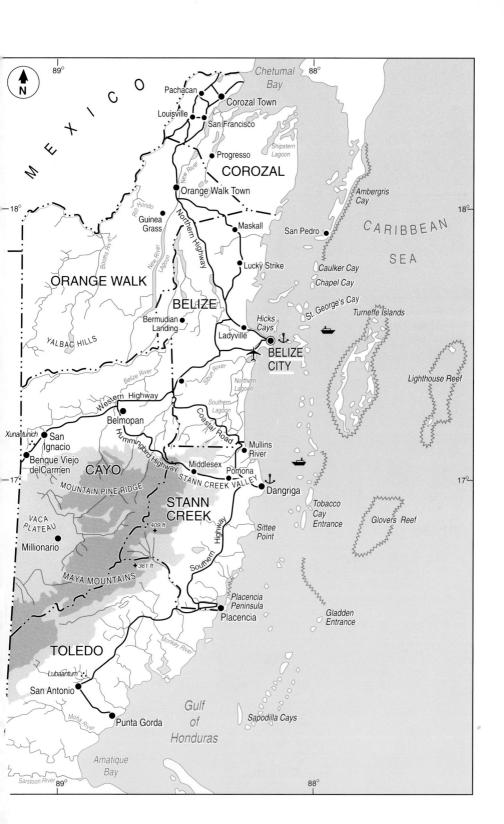

of Independence * 1980s: civil wars in Central America lead to massive influx of Central American refugees into Belize * 1991: Belize becomes full member of Organization of American States (OAS) * 1993: announcement of withdrawal of British armed forces * 1990s: economic citizenship programs target Taiwanese and Hong Kong nationals * 1998: First election contested by PUP without George Price as leader.

Constitution: Belize's head of state is the British monarch, who is represented in Belize by the Governor-General, who must be Belizean. The Prime Minister and Cabinet form the Executive. There is a National Assembly of two houses; an elected 29-member House of Representatives and a Senate of eight appointed members. Five of the Senators are appointed on the advice of the Prime Minister, two on the advice of the Leader of the Opposition, and one after consultation with the Belize Advisory Council. The Speaker of the House of Representatives and the President of the Senate may be non-members of the respective houses, when they would be ex-officio members. The maximum term of government is five years, although elections may be held earlier at the Prime Minister's dis-

cretion. The voting system is of single-member constituencies in which members are elected by simple majority. Belize District is governed by a nine-member elected council, while the others have seven-member elected councils. The six-member Belize Advisory Council is appointed for up to ten years by the Governor-General on the advice of the Prime Minister. The Leader of the Opposition must be consulted about the nominations and has the right of veto over two of them. The Council advises the Governor-General in the exercise of the prerogative of mercy and other matters. The Council may also act as a senior public service tribunal.

There are six judicial districts, in which courts of summary jurisdiction deal with criminal cases and district courts with civil cases. Courts are presided over by magistrates. Indictable cases are tried by jury in the Supreme Court. There is a National Appeal Court, with the Judicial Committee of the Privy Council in the UK acting as the final court of appeal.

Head of State: Queen Elizabeth II represented by Dr. Colville Young, Governor-General since 1993.

Main political groupings: There have been 4 elections since independence in 1981. In December 1984, the United Democratic Party

(UDP) won 21 of the 28 seats. In September 1989, the Peoples United Party (PUP) regained power, winning 15 seats to the UDP's 13. The UDP returned to power in the 1993 elections, despite two of its members breaking away to form a new party, the National Alliance for Belizean Reconstruction (NABR). NABR supported the UDP, allowing it to control 16 seats to the PUP's 13 in the enlarged House of Representatives. In the 1998 elections, the PUP won 26 out of 29 seats.

Armed forces: Until 1993 Britain maintained an army garrison in Belize as a deterrent to Guatemala's invasion plans. The 1,200 army and 800 RAF personnel, along with the fleet of Harrier aircraft, were finally withdrawn in 1994 when defense responsibility was formally handed over to the Belize Defence Force (BDF). Britain still maintains an army training facility in Belize—the British Army Training Support Unit Belize (BATSUB)—and has been providing technical assistance to the BDF. The BDF has limited manpower and equipment: 950 members, a maritime wing of 50, an air wing of 15, 8 maritime craft, 2 training aircraft, 6 mortars and 8 84mm weapons.

Membership of international organizations: United Nations and UN organizations, Caribbean Community

(Caricom), Organization of American States (OAS), Inter-American Development Bank (IDB) , British Commonwealth, African Caribbean and Pacific (ACP) States.

Media and communications: Belize currently has 4 weekly national newspapers, and 4 national radio stations as well as a number of local newspapers and radio stations. The radio stations include the privately owned Radio Krem and Love FM and Friends FM, which is run by the Broadcasting Corporation of Belize, a government controlled broadcasting organization. Belize has two local television stations—Channel 5 and Channel 7—which both broadcast a nightly news wrap up. They also both run weekly interview shows—Channel 5's *One-on-One*, and *Straight Talk* on Channel 7. There is very little else on television that is produced locally and the rest of the output of the two local channels consists of imported programs, mainly from the U.S. 80% of homes have radio and 62% have television.

Telecommunication services are provided by the privately owned Belize Telecommunication Limited, which has a good national network, including cellular service in most areas, e-mail and internet facilities, and community telephones in rural villages.

ECONOMY

GDP (1997): $618m.
GDP per capita (1997): $2,704.
Unit of currency: Belize $ (B$). 1U.S.$=2B$. Fixed exchange rate.
Inflation (%): 1.4 (1993), 2.6 (1994), 2.8 (1995), 6.4 (1996), 1.1 (1997).
GDP growth (%): 4.2 (1993), 2.6 (1994), 3.9 (1995), 1.4 (1996), 3.8 (1997).
GDP by sector (1997): Agriculture, fisheries and forestry 22.1%, commerce and trade 25.0%, manufacturing and mining 17.2%, transportation and communication 14.7%, construction 5.2%.
Fiscal deficit as % of GDP: 6.3 (1993), 6.4 (1994), 3.4 (1995), 0.8 (1996), 1.0 (1997).
Foreign debt (1997): $340m.
Foreign debt servicing as % of exports (1996): 12.8
Development aid per inhab-

itant (US$): 148 (1993), 139 (1994), 75 (1995)
Working population (1996): 75,500: agriculture 22.5%, wholesale and retail trade 15.4%, manufacturing 9.7%, education and health 9.2%, public administration 7.8%, construction 6.6%.
Unemployment (1997): 12.7%
Exports (1997): $159m.: sugar 29%, citrus concentrate 15.2%, bananas 16.5%, garments 11.7%, marine products 11%, other 16.6%.
Imports (1997): US$286m: machinery and equipment 25.8%, manufactures 18.3%, food 15.8%, fuels 12.9%, chemicals 10.9%, other 16.3%.
Trade balance (US$m): -75.4 (1994), -66.1 (1995), 53 (1996), 95 (1997).
Principal trading partners (1997): exports to U.S. 42.3%, UK 41.6%, other European Union 5.4%, Mexico 3.6%, Canada 2.6% Caricom 1.8%, other 2.6%.
Imports from U.S. 55.1%, Mexico 12.1%, UK 4.7%, Caricom 3.9%, other European Union 3.1%, Canada 1.6%, other 19.5%.
Belize runs trading surpluses with the UK, European Union and Canada. But with its other trading partners, it runs large trade deficits, which more than offset the surpluses. By far the largest trading deficit is with the U.S., accounting for 71% of Belize's total trade deficit in 1996. Belize has covered part of its growing trade deficit by increasing exploitation of preferential marketing agreements with the UK under the European Union's Lomé Agreeement. Between 1986 and 1996 exports to the UK

increased by 175% while imports rose by only 20%. On the other hand, during the same period exports from Belize to the U.S. rose by 38%, while imports from the U.S. into Belize rose 101%. Belize has also increased its imports from Caricom, Central America and Mexico significantly without a corresponding increase in exports.

BELIZE AND THE UNITED STATES/UK

Links between Britain and Belize remain even after the British army base closed in 1994. The British army still has a security and training role in Belize, and has been working closely with the Belize Defence Force. Apart from the security involvement, the major remaining link between Britain and Belize has been its aid program, which is most visible in the work of the volunteer sending agencies, Voluntary Service Overseas (VSO) and Raleigh International. The British government supports both these initiatives—VSO sends about 30 British professionals every year to assist Belizean organizations, and Raleigh organizes aid and adventure expeditions for about 400 young people every year. Both organizations are, however, phasing out their work in Belize, recognizing the ability of Belizean professionals and volunteers to operate at least as effectively as their British counterparts. The 1990s mark

the coming to an end of significant British involvement in Belize. While Britain's overall aid package to Belize is still substantial, this is because of outstanding commitments, specifically to improving road infrastructure. Once these obligations are met it is likely that British support to Belize will be significantly reduced, and aid contributions will instead be channeled through multilateral aid programs, most notably the European Union's.

Despite its lukewarm support for independence, the economic and political power of the U.S. wielded in such close proximity has inevitably meant that the U.S. has come to play a dominant role in Belize. Economically, the U.S. is Belize's most important trading partner, though Belize actually runs a large trade deficit with the U.S. and Belize still relies heavily on the European preferential marketing agreements to help

fund its trade imbalance. As USAID closed its Belize office in 1996, US aid to Belize is now channeled through multilateral organizations such as the World Bank and Inter-American Development Bank, through the Inter-American Foundation, or through the U.S. military. As with the British, U.S. aid also has a highly visible volunteer sending agency, the Peace Corps, which annually deploys 40 volunteer professionals in Belize. There are also strong links between U.S. and Belizean educational institutions and many Belizeans undertake studies in the U.S. The most obvious signs of U.S. culture in Belize are street fashions, which reflect the popularity of U.S. basketball (particularly the NBA), and black American music and dance. These fashions are not only found among the Creole youth of Belize City, but also in remote rural villages, which reflects the all-pervasive nature of this imported culture.